ASSET PROTECTION SECRETS

How America's Affluent Lawsuit Proof Their Wealth...

And How You Can Too!

REVISED EDITION

Hillel L. Presser, Esq., MBA

BROOKLINE PRESS, LLC

www.BrooklinePress.com

info@BrooklinePress.com

© 2013 Brookline Press, LLC

Published by

Brookline Press, LLC

800 Fairway Drive, Suite 340

Deerfield Beach, Florida 33441

Telephone: 561-953-1322

Fax: 561-953-1940

E-mail: info@BrooklinePress.com

Website: www.BrooklinePress.com

This book is designed to provide accurate and authoritative information on the subject of asset protection. It is sold with the understanding that neither the author nor the publisher is engaged in rendering legal, accounting, or other professional advice. As each individual situation is unique, questions specific to your circumstances should be addressed to an appropriate professional to ensure that your situation has been evaluated carefully and appropriately. The author and the publisher specifically disclaim any liability or loss incurred as a consequence, directly or indirectly, of using and applying any of the concepts in this book.

ISBN: 978-0-9886710-1-0

YOU COULD BE THE NEXT TARGET

THAT'S WHY YOU MUST ACT NOW TO:

- Protect your assets against lawsuits and other financial threats.
- Achieve lifetime financial security for yourself and for your family!

Presser has taken asset protection to the next level with Asset Protection Secrets. This book is packed with those little secrets litigation attorneys do not want us to know. Every one, rich or not, can use this text to shelter life's endeavors.

-Elizabeth Hickman, Florida

Very informative and easy to understand literature! This book is definitely helping me make more educated decisions regarding my assets.

- Brandon Miltsch, Georgia

I highly recommend Asset Protection Secrets (Revised Edition). I was able to implement some of this book's concepts the very next day in my own life.

- Chris Nichols, Florida

ACKNOWLEDGEMENTS

This book is dedicated to the loving memory of my grandparents, Florence and Sidney. I'd also like to extend deep gratitude to my parents, Stephen and Suzanne, as well as my sister, Shifra and grandmother, Marcia for all the love and support they've shown me throughout the years. Although I've come a long way since I left upstate New York, I felt that you were all with me throughout my journey.

Thanks to my wife Ashley for her unconditional love and support. Words can't express how much I appreciate you. You're truly my best friend.

Last, but not least; thanks to all my clients who have helped me as much as I have helped them.

COMMIT TO YOUR FINANCIAL SECURITY TODAY...
TOMMOROW MAY BE TOO LATE!

Call Today 561-953-1050

or visit: www.AssetProtectionAttorneys.com

Put the ideas in this book to work for you. And to help you, I offer you a complimentary Financial Self-Defense preliminary consultation. This includes a personal conversation with me to evaluate your risk and financial exposure. To register for a complimentary preliminary consultation, please contact me via phone 561-953-1050, via website www.AssetProtectionAttorneys.com or via email info@AssetProtectionAttorneys.com. Call us today, tomorrow may be too late!

I would be pleased to discuss your situation, explain my services and how we can work together to achieve your goals. There's no cost or obligation for this preliminary, confidential consultation. I accept clients nationwide – both individuals and companies.

In addition to a complimentary preliminary consultation, I am offering a complimentary asset protection Monthly Newsletter subscription to those who email info@AssetProtectionAttorneys.com and mention the "Asset Protection Newsletter." The Monthly Newsletter contains **educational** information regarding asset protection such as Q and A's, changes in law, trending articles and more.

Finally, I will be holding in person and online workshops, seminars and webinars to educate the public on asset protection tactics and self-defense strategies. Please email The Presser Law Firm, P.A. and mention that you are "interested in learning more about our workshops and seminars" to be given dates and locations for upcoming workshops in your area or to book me for an **educational** seminar or speaking engagement at one of your upcoming events.

TABLE OF CONTENTS

Introduction

When someone else is sued, it is a statistic. When you are sued, it's a nightmare. We know. For many years our firm, The Presser Law Firm, P.A. has protected the wealth of thousands of people against lawsuits and other financial dangers. Believe us. Even one lawsuit can financially destroy you. And it can happen when you least expect it!

It's not only the rich and famous who get sued. So do thousands of ordinary folks who had only hoped to build some financial security for themselves and their families. But their lives changed with one lawsuit. You too, undoubtedly, know people who were financially devastated by at least one financial disaster. If it happens to *others,* it *can* happen to *you!*

Many now poorer but wiser folks called us for help, but it was oftentimes too late. The sheriff had earlier auctioned their home, carted away their furniture or seized their bank account. It was too late to protect them. Those more forward-thinking folks protected their wealth *before* they were sued. They remained relatively unscathed by their legal problems. Still, few people seriously think about protecting their assets *until* they are sued. That's unfortunate. Sadly, only one in ten Americans has lawsuit protection – aside from their liability insurance.

Why, we wonder, do so many successful people who carefully scrutinize every business deal, demand the best business and investment advice, and even micro-plan their vacations, do absolutely nothing to fortify their wealth against the countless financial pitfalls they surely will someday encounter? Procrastination is their deadly enemy!

Think about it. A million lawyers hunt for lawsuit defendants. They and their litigious clients are a clear and real danger to *anyone* who has exposed assets. America is the world's lawsuit capital. And you don't have to do anything wrong to get sued – and lose. You may be in the wrong place at the wrong time and *your* wealth can be lost! Nor can you predict what you might lose in a lawsuit. Plaintiffs with minimal injury pocket millions in punitive damages. One defective product or class action lawsuit can bankrupt your business. That's why most lawsuits settle. No defendant can go to trial certain of winning. Nor can they foresee how much they can lose. So plaintiffs' lawyers use lawsuits to extort whopping settlements and defendants with exposed wealth pay huge settlements because they cannot afford to gamble in court.

The lawsuit, of course, is only one path to financial ruin. Life's a financial minefield. For example, you can be happily married today and divorce next year. What would you then lose?

About two million Americans will file bankruptcy this year and most of these people will lose *everything* they own. No, you can't always foresee your financial problems, yet bad things happen to all of us: a lost job, medical bills, a sour business deal. You've heard the stories.

The bottom line: Shelter your wealth! Think defensively and realistically! Don't ask *whether* – but *when* – *you'll* get hit with a serious financial problem. How can you fortify yourself from that eventuality?

How This Book Will Help You

Because so many people have exposed, *vulnerable* wealth, our goal through this interview is to tell you how you can lawsuit-proof yourself and gain lifelong financial security. This security is now enjoyed by so many of our clients, seminar attendees and readers of our other financial self-defense titles and the information from this book can benefit you.

This book *can* give you and your family lifetime peace of mind. You surely want the confidence that you won't lose your wealth – regardless of your financial or legal problems. That's the books aim. You'll also see how you can discourage and even stop pending lawsuits. Prevent even *one* lawsuit and you'll recover many times the fees you'll spend to protect yourself. Become lawsuit-proof and you can negotiate settlement from a position of strength because you have less to lose and your opponent less to gain. Asset protection levels the litigation playing field. Get that edge!

Who Needs This Book?

Quite a few folks need the information that this book presents. If you have valuable assets, you need this book. Perhaps you only have a few dollars in the bank, a modest home equity or a small retirement account. You worked hard for what you now own and won't easily recover from a major financial setback. So you'll find this book vital whether you have significant or negligible assets. Also, read it whether you are now totally exposed to lawsuits or *think* you're already well-protected. We'll explain how to shelter your assets from scratch, as well as how to improve your present protection. And you'll find these strategies vital to you whether you have never before been sued, are now defending yourself against a lawsuit, or have been sued and want better future protection. You'll also find helpful information whether your goal is to protect *your* own wealth or a clients'. (Yes, financial advisors, accountants and lawyers *must* help safeguard their clients' finances.) Whether you're just starting out, want to shield future wealth, your nest egg, or your children's inheritance, the techniques we will discuss in these pages can show you how to protect yourself against virtually *any* financial threat. You'll also find advanced strategies that can protect your business or professional practice as well.

How to Use This Book

A warning here: This is *not* a do-it-yourself guide. Asset protection is too complex. Do not attempt to do it on your own without expert guidance. As your tax, insurance and financial advisors assist you on planning issues that involve *their* expertise you'll need an asset protection specialist to guide you to the most effective ways to shield your wealth. Our goal with this book is to familiarize you with the more common protective strategies, tactics and tools. Still, no book can provide more than an overview. We can say far more about any one strategy; and each strategy is only one of many. Further any one strategy may – or may not – be right for your situation. Moreover, lawsuit-proofing often combines strategies to maximize protection. So this book presents only the possibilities. Your professional advisor must design *your* best plan.

Here's a brief preview about what you'll find within this book. Chapter 1 gives an overview of asset protection. Chapter 2 focuses on the planning process and how to customize *your* best plan. Chapter 3 discusses the numerous entities and strategies commonly used today to protect assets. Chapters 4-10 explore the different methods to protect specific assets. Chapter 11 discusses various self-defense tactics that you can use in special situations. The final chapter explains how to get started on your own wealth protection program.

You'll find many different concepts in this book. Some you're probably familiar with. Others will be new. If you now use some of these strategies, you'll better understand why and how they work. But here's another word of caution: Asset protection planning also brings uncertain outcomes. No one strategy may completely safeguard you. And each has tax and other financial consequences. Protection planning – as with other legal or financial plans – has many possible game plans. This book presents the more effective and more frequently used firewalls, that if timely applied, may prevent loss of your assets. Our other books on asset protection expand on these strategies, some from different perspectives. So educate yourself! Read these books! Learn more about asset protection as you do other aspects of your financial planning. We recommend: *So Sue Me: How to Protect Your Assets from the Lawsuit Explosion, Financial Self-Defense* and *Asset Protection: A Guide for Professionals and Their Clients*. These helpful guides are available from Brookline Press, LLC www.BrooklinePress.com.

We hope that this book helps you in your financial planning. We certainly appreciate the opportunity that the Financial Forum has given us to express our views on this very important topic.

1

Asset

Protection

Basics

Tell us why asset protection is so important today?

The answer is obvious. We live in a lawsuit-crazy, financially risky world; where too many people unexpectedly lose their assets. More and more families, individuals and businesses are sued each year. It can happen to *anyone*! That's why so many people today want and need to protect their wealth against lawsuits and these other dangers. They want financial security. They want peace of mind. They want and need to know how to defend themselves financially. This is vital for people from every economic background. That's why asset protection is such a hot topic today, and that's why our services are in such great demand.

What is 'asset protection'?

Asset protection is simply adopting a range of strategies to title your home, savings, real property, business and other assets in a manner that legally shields them against lawsuits and other claims. The goal to protect one's assets from litigants and creditors might seem apparent, yet there is more to it. Asset protection – or lawsuit-proofing, as some call it – creates a safety net. It won't guarantee that you'll avoid lawsuits or other financial calamities, but it *can* guarantee you'll lose fewer assets if you do run into trouble. Unless your assets are protected, you're in 'free-fall.' You're vulnerable and exposed. You can't afford that exposure. Not with the many risks you'll encounter.

Of course, there are other threats to one's wealth. Inflation, recession, stock market downturns, the devaluation of the dollar and other economic risks – can also eradicate one's wealth. But we leave the solutions to those problems to financial planners and other professionals. Ours is a different niche. Our job is to protect our clients' wealth against direct predatory attack.

How bad is the litigation problem in America?

It has reached epidemic proportion. About 100 million lawsuits are filed every year. Statistically, each American will be sued five times over their lifetime. And this doesn't include all the other potential threats – divorce, foreclosure, etc. Today, the challenge is not making money – it's keeping it!

Why is America so lawsuit crazy? Sociologists, economists, politicians, and lawyers each have their own theories. Our perception is that we have too many lawyers, too many laws, and too few judges with the courage or common sense to summarily throw out the blatantly frivolous lawsuits. We also have too many juries that don't rule on the basis of liability. Their goal is to empty a defendant's 'deep pockets' and redistribute the wealth.

There are also too many incentives to sue. For example, a punitive damage claim can enrich a plaintiff who has little or no actual damage with a multi-million-dollar windfall. Nor are there many reasons *not* to sue. It won't cost a plaintiff a dime in legal fees because most lawyers work for a contingent fee.

There is much wrong with our legal system, but it is not only the system's fault, as perverse as it is. The fault is chiefly that as a society we have become a nation of victims. When things go wrong – as they invariably do – we instinctively point blame elsewhere. The lawsuit is the natural consequence of this distorted national mindset.

Walter K. Olson's, *The Litigation Explosion* explains, our litigation dilemma from a different perspective:

"The unleashing of litigation in its full fury has done cruel, grave harm and little lasting good. It has helped sunder some of the most sensitive and profound relationships of human life: Between the parents who have nurtured a child; between the healing professions and those whose life and well-being are entrusted to their care. It clogs and jams the gears of commerce, sowing friction and distrust between the productive enterprises on which material progress depends and on all who buy their products, work at their plants and offices or join in their undertakings. It seizes on former love and intimacy as raw materials to be transmuted into hatred and estrangement. It exploits the bereavement that some day awaits the survivors of us all and turns it to an unending source of poisonous recrimination. It torments the provably innocent and rewards the palpably irresponsible. It devours hard-won savings and worsens every animosity of a diverse society. It is the special American burden, the one feature hardly anyone admires of a society that is otherwise envied the world around."

Amen!

It sounds like you have an axe to grind against the tort lawyers.

No. It's just that we are passionate about what we do. With so many lawyers around, it is inevitable that there are so many lawsuits. The thought of nearly a million lawyers running around searching for their next victim endangers anyone with significant assets. You can't blame every lawyer, though. Not every lawyer is in the lawsuit business. And if you look hard you can still find plaintiffs' lawyers who won't file a frivolous lawsuit. They use their good judgment and do not abuse the judicial system. We are proud to be part of the legal profession with *these* lawyers as our colleagues. But how many lawyers *do* throw lawsuits around like confetti? How many lawyers see the lawsuit as a way to make a fast buck? How many lawyers *don't* care if their lawsuit is meritless as long as they can extort enough money from some hapless defendant to make the lawsuit worthwhile? Too many!

Apparently, the tide has turned. The *American Bar Association Journal* (the largest US publication for lawyers) in its article *Protect Your Assets Before A Lawsuit Arises* counsels their 400,000 members that asset protection is as critical for *them* as to their clients. One trial lawyer interviewed for the article frankly admits, "I don't want people doing to me what I do to other people all day in court." So, in a sense, by defending the wealth of prospective lawsuit targets we believe we are helping to counteract a bad system that favors bad lawsuits.

Isn't asset protection only for the wealthy?

That's a fallacy. It's true that America's wealthiest families were traditionally 'the deep pocket' defendants who were most concerned about shielding their wealth. The social elites of past eras sheltered their massive wealth with trusts, family corporations and other protective entities to privatize or lawsuit-proof their property; however, they seldom referred to their financial strategies as 'asset protection'. But the super-rich are no longer the only lawsuit targets. Virtually every American with *any* assets now needs protection. So asset protection *isn't* only for the affluent. In fact, most of our clients have only modest wealth. However, their modest wealth is precious to *them*! That's what counts.

How would you feel if you lost *your* assets; your home, car, savings? Wealth is relative. It is not only the rich and affluent who need protection. Anyone with *any* assets needs protection!

Here's an example. An airport shoe-shiner was sued for $100,000 on a bank loan he guaranteed for his son. He owned only his Bronx home with a $100,000 equity. Many people don't consider $100,000 serious wealth. They would hate to lose it, but this loss wouldn't hurt their lifestyle. That's not how our shoe-shine client saw it. His $100,000 home equity was his entire life savings. How many more shoes must

4

he shine to replace his $100,000? He will have a harder time recouping his $100,000 than a millionaire would his millions. That's why we take *every* case serious.

But isn't asset protection less important for people in safe occupations?

You would think so, but that's not necessarily true. The unfortunate reality is that no matter how safe and secure we think we are, we are each exposed to liability and financial hazards, regardless of our lifestyle, occupation, or how carefully we live our lives. You can minimize the dangers but you can't entirely avoid them. In our litigious society there are too many opportunities to encounter trouble. What financial trouble awaits you next month, or next year? Who knows when they might get hit with a costly accident or negligence claim, a lawsuit for breach of contract or professional malpractice, creditor claims from a failed business or divorce? You see the point. The potential liabilities are limitless. But until trouble strikes, you don't realize your vulnerability. And until you recognize your vulnerability, you may take your financial stability for granted. That's unfortunate. And dangerous! You must think defensively. People shouldn't ask *if* they will someday face financial danger. They should ask *when* and *how* will it happen! Since they can't predict the answer, their only logical option is to build the strongest protective fortress possible for their wealth *before* trouble strikes.

We sometimes learn that lesson too late. One of our clients claimed she would never be sued because she was a schoolteacher. True, she wasn't sued for her teaching, but a year later she *was* sued for over a million dollars for the negligent handling of her mother's estate. Obviously, a lawsuit need not relate to your employment. No matter how cautious and careful you are you still can get sued. For instance, anyone who drives could get into an accident. We are all at risk. It is not only doctors, real estate developers, or business owners who attract lawsuits. *Everyone* is a potential target!

Everybody seemingly wants a piece of the action and a chance to win the legal lottery. Kids sue parents, partners sue partners, patients sue doctors, customers sue manufacturers, students sue teachers, and parishioners sue their clergy. From toddlers to executors of the deceased, anyone can sue and nobody is immune – not even the President of the United States.

Perhaps more frightening than the blizzard of lawsuits is the number of ridiculous cases that squeeze their way through the court system and reach a jury. It seems that the more ridiculous the case, the greater the plaintiff's victory. Scan the newspapers and magazines. Watch TV. Laugh to the Saturday night stand-up comics. Who can most scintillate us with the day's craziest lawsuit? Why has litigation become our favorite form of entertainment?

Think for a moment, though: Are these cases really humorous when you consider the great waste of time, money, and energy that was expended to defend against them? Are these frivolous and bizarre cases truly funny when you consider the aggravation, worry, and grief that so many defendants were forced to endure before they could shake themself free of these nutty litigants and their stupid lawsuits? Some of these whacky plaintiffs actually *won* their cases, which bolsters our argument that our legal system is only a legal lottery where even a bad case has a good chance.

You might argue that these cases are anomalies and rare curiosities within our legal system, but you would be wrong. Hundreds or thousands of equally ridiculous cases are now pending in your local courthouse. We know. We see enough ludicrous cases in our own practice. Take a few minutes to read the weekly Bar Journals for equally far-fetched cases breaking new legal grounds. There's always a picture of another grinning, victorious plaintiff's lawyer who bagged another defendant on some spurious grounds.

As we say, you do not have to do anything wrong to be sued and lose. You only have to be in the wrong place at the wrong time or somehow come across some greedy lunatic who thinks he or she has reason to be grieved. Voilá! *Your* wealth could soon be in *their* pocket!

But isn't it true that most lawsuits involve small amounts of money and
are not wealth threatening?

That's true to a point. If a credit card company sues you for $6000, you only have $6000 at risk. But even when you can endure the odds of being sued and the uncertainty of winning or losing, you must consider the possibility of a devastating award. You can't predict what you could lose in a major lawsuit. A plaintiff who wins a few dollars in actual damages may pocket millions more in punitive damages. A buyer of a $20 defective product can turn it into a class action case that can cost the seller millions – or billions. One lawsuit can start an avalanche of others. Enough nonsense lawsuits can topple the most powerful business or wealthiest family, as we have seen with litigation against tobacco, pharmaceuticals, asbestos and other industries.

This uncertainty of outcome also explains why nine out of ten lawsuits settle. What defendant can go to trial confident of victory? What defendant can know what they may lose if their case goes to trial? How many defendants can afford the exorbitant legal fees to answer these questions? So plaintiffs' lawyers use lawsuits as their weapons to extort whopping settlements because the economics are always with the plaintiffs. The defendant is coerced to pay 'go away' money, because the defendant who has exposed wealth simply has too much to lose by gambling on litigation.

Of course, lawsuits can involve more than money. A lawsuit can attack your personal character – particularly those that allege fraud, racketeering, or conspiracy. And you may have good cause to get angry when a lawsuit attacks your professional competency. Ask any doctor how it feels to be characterized in a malpractice lawsuit as 'negligent, incompetent or reckless.'

One leading New York thoracic surgeon was sued twice in his thirty-year career but will tell you, "You know you did nothing wrong, but you begin to question your own competence. Inevitably your self-confidence and self-esteem drops a few notches."

Every lawsuit creates some stress and uneasiness; however, a major lawsuit can disrupt your social relationships, cloud your thoughts, dampen your enthusiasm for the future, and always create that nagging sense of insecurity. The essence of the lawsuit was best voiced by the *Tort Informer:* "The law provides incredible financial incentives to seek out a victim with deep pockets, drag him into court, ruin his reputation, wear him down with endless discovery demands, pay a fortune to defend himself and then extort a settlement. This is not justice in any sense of the word." But if you are well-protected you may avoid all this. That's our goal with our clients.

If I have liability insurance, do I still need an asset protection plan?

That's an excellent question. Let's put it in perspective. Liability insurance is important, but liability insurance can't replace the other ways to protect yourself. Liability insurance insures only one in three lawsuits. So most lawsuits *aren't* covered. For example, you may be sued for breach of contract, a defaulted loan, or family dispute. The possibilities of an *uninsured* claim are endless. Nor does insurance *fully* cover every claim. How good is your million-dollar liability policy if you're sued for two million? And with today's unpredictable, ludicrous jury awards, who can be certain they won't be hit with an excessive judgment? Nor can you overlook those countless policy exclusions and loopholes. You can't even be certain that your insurance company will be in business when you're hit with a claim? Insurance companies – like other companies – do go bankrupt. We strongly recommend buying liability insurance. It's a smart first step for protection and risk management. Also buy as much liability insurance as you can reasonably afford. But make liability insurance *only* your starting point. It can't replace a solid asset protection plan that will fully protect you against *every* size and type claim.

A lot of people might question whether it is legal to shield their assets against lawsuits and creditors. Can you comment on this?

It's not only legal but essential! What thinking person could today question the legality of asset protection planning? And who could question its necessity? Yes, there can be that troublesome grey area that separates legal from illegal asset protection

8

planning. And you can't cross the line. For example, a legal plan won't involve secrecy, concealing assets, perjury, tax fraud, money laundering or bankruptcy fraud. That's not what asset protection is about. You want *legal* protection. A questionable 'protective' strategy can only get you into bigger trouble. If you question the legitimacy of a proposed plan, talk to another planner. There are many perfectly legitimate ways to shield your wealth without engaging in dubious or downright illegal practices. If you incorrectly assume that asset protection involves secrecy, tax evasion, concealing assets or other questionable practices, then read this book again. We discuss *only* 100 percent legal techniques.

The legitimacy of asset protection planning is best evidenced by the many trade and scholastic books now available on the topic. Many journals and articles openly discuss – and recommend – asset protection. The American Bar Association has formed an asset protection subcommittee. Those who equate asset protection with sleazy practices simply don't understand the field.

We might explain the legitimacy of asset protection as the intelligent application of the many statutory and common law tools – exemption laws, co-ownerships, corporations, LLCs, trusts, bankruptcy and so forth – to best shield one's wealth. We didn't create these tools. We only show our clients how to use them to their advantage.

Given that asset protection is legal – what about the ethics or morality of preventing creditors from getting paid?

The moral or ethical issues are another question. Some people believe it's unethical or improper to shelter their assets from those who have a rightful claim. But these folks might then think about asset protection as financial self-defense to discourage frivolous and harassing lawsuits and to make them a less likely lawsuit target. They'll live life more confident about their financial security. Of course, one can always pay or favorably settle those claims they feel morally obliged to pay, and our clients oftentimes do – to assuage their conscience. And that's their prerogative. But if they're unprotected, they have no choice. They can be wrongfully stripped of their wealth. That's what we want to prevent.

We can better make the case that those who *don't* safeguard their families' security are negligent, and in breach of their own self-obligation. Likewise are their lawyers who defend them on a serious case and never suggest that they fortify their assets in the event they lose their lawsuit. Yet few defense lawyers offer such common sense advice. It's sad. Inevitably their clients pay the price for their lack of common sense.

We can also look at the ethics of asset protection from another perspective. Is it unethical to file bankruptcy to eliminate debt? Is it unethical to use corporations or limited liability companies to limit your personal exposure from business debts? Is it unethical to keep your home or retirement accounts that may be exempt from creditor seizure? Most people would think not because the law makes it permissible. Asset protection planners only take advantage of the statutory and case law that in one way or another shields assets. But ultimately, whether or not to pay a claim must be left to the client's conscience.

Aside from not losing your assets to lawsuits are there other benefits of asset protection planning?

That's another important question. When you protect your assets, you gain four big benefits. First, it will discourage lawsuits and help you to more favorably settle any pending lawsuits. Second, it can lower or eliminate your insurance costs. Third, it improves your overall financial planning, and finally, and most importantly, it prevents the loss of your assets if a claim is made against you. Those are indeed four powerful benefits. But the biggest benefit is that you get peace of mind. You will sleep nights. You worry less about losing your wealth. That's what our clients want!

I imagine that a major lawsuit can cause quite a bit of stress. How do most of your clients react to litigation?

Who can be happy about being a defendant in a major lawsuit? It can be emotionally devastating. They can spend years and hundreds of thousands of dollars – or even millions – to defend the case. We have seen our share of nervous breakdowns, divorces, health problems and personal bankruptcies triggered by litigation. And how our clients responds to the stresses of litigation can influence the outcome of their case even more than their asset protection plan. We have had many clients settle their cases for more than was necessary only because they could no longer endure the emotional strain from the lawsuit. Their own emotional fragility was the weak link in their protective armor. But we well-understand this and we spend a fair amount of our time responding to our clients' stresses. Ultimately, the client's ability to withstand the strain of conflict determines how far we may go with a case.

How does asset protection discourage lawsuits?

The most effective way to discourage litigation is to convince a potential plaintiff that you have no exposed wealth that they can seize even if they sue and win their case. By discouraging litigation you avoid the time, hassle and expense of defending against the lawsuit. Isn't it better to discourage a lawsuit than to be forced to defend against the lawsuit and spend huge legal fees, time, and effort to 'win'? If you prevent even one potential lawsuit, you pay for your asset protection plan many times over.

Litigation is economics. A plaintiff's lawyer evaluates the case against you and weighs the cost of suing against the odds of winning. The lawyer then factors in the likely recovery based on your *exposed* assets. Essentially, the lawyer decides *are you worth suing?* Few sensible plaintiffs sue when they cannot foresee recovering enough to make the lawsuit worthwhile. Of course, you may nevertheless get sued because even a shaky lawsuit has some 'settlement value.' Most people will pay something to make their lawsuits disappear. This legal 'extortion' is one reason people dislike lawyers and litigants; nevertheless, it's reality. It's 'part of the game.' People also sue 'vindictively'. They have a score to settle. There are other reasons why even those well-protected get sued. You may be a peripheral defendant in a lawsuit. Your assets aren't investigated because you're one of many defendants. But as a rule, it's not whether you have assets that determine whether you get sued; it's whether you have *exposed* assets. To avoid lawsuits, you must convince a prospective plaintiff that you have that *impregnable* financial fortress and they have nothing much to gain from suing.

Whenever one of our clients is threatened with litigation we try to 'sell' the adversary on the fact that our client is well-protected. We don't use an 'in-your face' approach, but we do quickly let the adversary know that even if he sues and wins, he has little chance of collecting. Why spend years in court only to end up empty handed? It usually works. Most legal threats then vanish or are quickly and inexpensively resolved. Lawsuit avoidance is a major part of our practice.

If I have a good asset protection plan, can I forego liability insurance?

We emphasize that we seldom suggest asset protection as a complete substitute for liability insurance. Nevertheless, certain high-risk professionals and businesses find their insurance costs prohibitive. Or liability insurance may not be available. Our asset protection plan then complements a low liability policy or substitutes for insurance. The problem with insurance is not only its cost, but that it also attracts litigants. Nevertheless, liability insurance is invaluable for most risk management programs. Cost-effective insurance should be your primary defensive barrier. But be sure to supplement it with an asset protection plan. A lawsuit defendant's strategy then is to settle a case within the policy limits and have the plaintiff forego further claim against the defendant's personal assets. You can achieve this only when your assets are well-protected.

A number of our clients – particularly physicians and manufacturers – 'go bare' or without insurance. Their insurance costs are simply too expensive. We then make certain they have the strongest defensive plan. Even in these cases we recommend a legal defense policy to cover their defense costs if they are sued. So in many instances, our asset protection plan can save a client tens – or hundreds of thousands – a year in insurance costs.

How can asset protection improve your other financial objectives?

Asset protection is only one financial goal. You must coordinate it with your estate planning, as well as your tax, investment and other financial goals. You want to create a comprehensive, integrated financial plan. For example, we integrate our client's asset protection with their estate plan. People who need asset protection often have no estate plan – not even a simple will. Their need for asset protection oftentimes prompts estate planning. And we can oftentimes accomplish creative results when we combine asset protection with estate planning. Asset protection plans might also offer legitimate tax benefits. For example, we may use the limited partnership to lawsuit-proof your assets but the limited partnership may also save you significant estate taxes. Of course, you want to avoid promoters who 'sell' asset protection through *illegal* tax schemes (pure trusts, etc.). And your planner should inform you about the tax and other financial consequences of any proposed plan. For an integrated, complex plan, you should involve your financial and estate planning professionals. They're essential members of the team. We encourage this team approach to our clients' planning – particularly those who have considerable assets or complex estates. Our clients are quite satisfied when we plan their finances together with their other advisors. They then feel that their several financial concerns have been fully addressed and coordinated.

That brings us to the question of cost. How costly is a good asset protection plan?

Protecting your assets is not too costly. And it probably won't take more than several hours of your time. The average family can usually gain good protection for a few thousand dollars, sometimes less. We frequently shelter large fortunes for less than a fraction of what their investment advisor charges each year, and many protective steps cost absolutely nothing. But you have to see it in perspective. A doctor and prospective client once complained to us that he did not have the spare cash to set up the few entities he needed to safeguard his $3 million net worth. He thought the proposed $15,000 fee was too costly. However, this doctor spends $65,000 a year for malpractice insurance. This $65,000 policy covers only malpractice claims – and only up to one million dollars per claim. Next year the doctor will pay another $65,000 (assuming his premiums don't increase) for the same limited protection. In comparison, we offered this physician *complete* protection against *any* lawsuit, in *any* amount, for the *rest of his life*, all for less than one-fourth the cost of what he pays each year for malpractice insurance. So which is the better deal – insurance or asset protection? Don't think of asset protection as an expense. It's an investment – and a great investment – if you want financial security!

You say the main goal of asset protection is to lawsuit-proof your wealth, but does it really work?

Yes. But as with most things, that answer has several qualifiers: Successful asset protection also depends on *ifs*. Asset protection works *if* you protect yourself *before* trouble strikes. It works *if* you use the right strategies and tools for your particular situation. It works *if* you have the right professional advisor. It works *if* you stay committed to continuously *sheltering* your wealth. The ultimate purpose of any asset protection plan, of course, is to *safeguard* your wealth under a worst-case scenario – you are sued and lose. And the odds are that you *will* someday lose a lawsuit, so you need well-protected assets. You must assume that *your* asset protection plan will someday be put to this test.

Of course, even when you are judgment-proof you can't easily ignore the problems from a judgment. A plaintiff's lawyer can stubbornly pursue the even well-protected defendant. And a plaintiff might seize *some* assets because you can't always protect every last asset. Some 'loose change', for one reason or another, becomes exposed.

Frequently, the benefit of well-protected assets is realized only after the plaintiff wins a judgment and has exhausted their collection remedies. Until then, some plaintiffs won't reasonably settle, despite assurances that the defendant is indeed judgment-proof. And *every* case has *some* settlement value, even when a plaintiff cannot seize the defendant's assets. Nobody wants a judgment pending against them for twenty or more years. And a judgment creditor may possibly petition a defendant into bankruptcy. Nor will an adverse judgment help one's credit rating. The ultimate success of an asset protection plan then is not whether the plaintiff recovered *something*. Most defendants pay *'something'* to end their case. Our goal is not to have our client lose *significant* assets. That's how we ultimately measure our success. We ask this one question: "What more could we – or anyone – have done to achieve a better outcome in this case?" That's our litmus test. Our plans invariably pass that test. Our clients lose few assets to litigation. Very few!

Can you give us an idea of what kind of people come to you to protect their assets?

We attract clients of virtually every age, net worth, occupation and geographic location. We may do a plan to protect a Bostonian millionaire in the morning and another plan in the afternoon to shelter a North Dakota wage-earner's assets. We meet a lot of interesting people from every background. Our client mix keeps our work exciting.

Obviously, a good many of our clients are physicians and other professionals, real estate professionals, business owners and others who are more likely lawsuit targets. The economic downturn now brings to us many real estate speculators, and homeowners who are 'upside-down' in their mortgages. They now want to protect their assets. We are also doing more planning for people with credit card and other general creditor problems. The fastest growing segment of our practice are those clients who want to lawsuit-proof their business and professional practice.

What types of cases might you not accept?

We are quite busy and therefore selective about accepting clients. First and foremost, we reject prospective clients who come to us for improper purposes. We don't want clients whose goal is to defraud clients, money launder, evade taxes or play other games. Our job is difficult enough and we don't need cases that involve improper objectives or means. Moreover, we won't accept cases that would assist, say, a divorced father from paying child support or defrauding a spouse in a divorce proceeding. We actually refuse quite a few prospects when we are not comfortable with the situation. We also have to have the right 'fit' with the client. Some prospects may have unrealistic expectations, not cooperate in implementing their plan, or are game-players. So there is a screening process, including background checks, before someone becomes a Presser Law Firm, P.A. client.

How many of your clients, in the final analysis, actually needed their asset protection plan?

They all needed it because not one could be certain trouble wouldn't someday strike. It's no different than buying insurance. You buy it with the hopes you won't need it. But if you do need it – it's there. Meanwhile, our clients know that they are safe – no matter what. Those who are unprotected can only hope.

2

Designing

Your Plan

Can you give us an overview on how you design an asset protection plan?

If you ask five attorneys this same question, you would get five different responses. The same could be said about asset protection. This "same question, different answer" phenomenon is partly due to the fact that laws constantly evolve and change; that asset protection is as much an art as a science; and that there is more than one way to effectively protect one's assets. Moreover, one must always consider the laws of the client's state as well as federal laws. Finally, no two clients or their situations are precisely the same. Still, some fundamental components are common to every sound asset protection program.

Asset protection is far more complex than most people, and even some planners would believe. The less effective planner will only address the "what do we do and how do we do it" aspects of asset protection. However, there are actually five dimensions that we must address in order to construct a truly effective plan: these are the What, When, How, Why and Where of asset protection.

The 'What' of asset protection covers what assets we wish to protect.

The 'When' of asset protection deals with when to implement a plan in relation to a creditor threat. If one implements a plan before creditors threaten, the plan may be relatively simple yet still effective to repel a future creditor attack.

Planning after storm clouds have gathered usually requires more sophisticated planning and often more extreme measures, and sometimes (depending on the circumstances) the plan has less likelihood to succeed. The 'When' of asset protection then primarily deals with Fraudulent Transfer Law.

The 'How' relates to how we implement the three core strategies. This book largely addresses the 'How' of asset protection. The 'How' of asset protection also deals with how we maintain a plan once it is in place.

The 'Why' of asset protection? In short, the best asset protection plans have an ostensible, viable, bona fide reason for being implemented other than asset protection itself. Asset protection is the icing on the cake, so to speak. Asset protection only for asset protection's sake may lead a judge to consider the planning an attempt to delay, defeat, or hinder a creditor, which is a violation of fraudulent transfer law. In this instance, the judge typically sets aside the plan, allowing a creditor to reach supposedly protected assets.

The 'Where' of asset protection deals with choice-of-law, conflict-of-law, and jurisdictional issues. For a sample jurisdictional issue, consider assets located outside the U.S. and outside the reach of a U.S. judge. An example of a choice-of-laws issue may be someone who sets up a Nevada corporation, with Nevada-based management, yet he and his assets are in Missouri. What laws will be used to determine how those assets are treated for debtor-creditor purposes when the stockholders are sued in Iowa? Finally, a conflict-of-laws issue could arise when a resident of a state (for example, Texas) is sued in federal court. Will Texas' unlimited homestead protection hold up when a Texas citizen is sued by the FTC in a federal suit? You can see that protecting one's assets takes considerable thought to handle the many variables.

Broadly speaking, how can someone lawsuit-proof their assets?

Let's start with the basics. To lawsuit-proof a client's assets, we would normally use one or more of three basic strategies. The first strategy is to own only *exempt* assets. The strategy here is to own as many assets as possible that are automatically protected from creditors under federal or state law. A surprising number of assets are automatically exempt or immune from creditor seizure. For example, your state law may *exempt* all or part of your home equity, retirement plan, insurance, annuities, wages and certain personal property. The converse objective is to own few or no assets that are not exempt and self-protected. We will later expand upon this exemption strategy through numerous examples.

The second strategy is to title *non-exempt or unprotected assets to one or more protective entities.* When you title your assets to one or more protective entities, a judgment creditor cannot seize those assets. We have many different protective entities and arrangements to choose from: co-ownerships, corporations, irrevocable trusts and COPE's (limited partnerships and limited liability companies), as well as numerous international or financial entities. We'll talk about these and other protective entities and strategies throughout our interview.

The third strategy is to fully *encumber* or *equity strip your assets.* The goal here is to reduce your assets' value to your creditor by mortgaging your exposed assets and protecting the proceeds. We'll also tell you about a number of different ways to accomplish this.

We often combine these strategies. For example, we may title an asset to a protective entity, then equity strip the same asset and invest the proceeds in an exempt asset or safekeep the proceeds in still another protective entity. Most plans involving significant assets combine these three strategies or 'firewalls,' as we call them. The possibilities are endless. And there are other strategies – usually more of a financial nature – that can also be blended into a plan.

Each of the above strategies fall into the category of either *transfer-based asset protection* or transferring an asset out of a creditor's reach, or *transformational asset protection* which is transforming the asset into something a creditor couldn't get or wouldn't want. For example, part of one's salary can be placed into an ERISA-governed plan (401(k), etc.) that is exempt from creditors. Although this involves exemption planning, it also involves transferring cash into an ERISA-governed plan, and is therefore transfer-based protection as well. Another method involves using

19

exposed cash to prepay certain expenses or repay favored creditors provided those creditors aren't 'insiders' under applicable fraudulent transfer or fraudulent conveyance law. For example, one could take exposed cash and use it to pay in advance for a 5-year commercial lease. Such techniques, which results in the right to use an asset – the leased property – which right most creditors wouldn't want, exemplifies transformational asset protection.

Nearly every asset protection strategy relies upon one or more of these three core strategies, which independently or simultaneously utilize either a transformational or a transfer-based methodology.

What specific asset protection tools or 'firewalls' do you use in your planning?

We have any number of specific protective firewalls, but we most commonly use these eight 'firewalls:' 1) federal and state exemptions, 2) co-ownerships, 3) corporations, 4) limited partnerships, 5) limited liability companies, 6) domestic trusts, 7) international entities, and 8) debt-shields (equity stripping).

Each specific firewall has its own unique characteristics, strengths and weaknesses, advantages and disadvantages, applications and instances where they would or wouldn't be useful. Think colors on the artist's palette. Some colors are more commonly used than others; however, each is vital to achieve artistic perfection. Still, that perfect portrait depends on their correct application. We'll talk more about each firewall so you can see how it might apply to the various assets.

Can other 'firewalls,' entities or tools also shield assets?

Of course. There are literally hundreds, or even thousands, of variations on the theme. There are many more entities we could discuss, but most entities and strategies, conceptually at least, fall within one of these 'firewall' categories. For example, limited liability partnerships and limited liability limited partnerships are variations on the limited partnership. The limited liability company also works in much the same way. Of course, we can't fully discuss *every* possible firewall. Nor should we get too technical. We only want to discuss the fundamentals or more common tools and strategies. More advanced methodologies may combine legal and financial strategies. These invariably complex arrangements can provide financial as well as protective benefits. Nor is asset protection planning static. We professional asset protection planners constantly invent new strategies and tactics. Every field is fast-changing. So is ours.

Some asset protection planners recommend only one specific entity or strategy for asset protection planning. Is one technique better than another?

Let's destroy that common myth. There's no such thing as a 'one-size fits all' asset protection plan. But you're right. Some 'so-called' asset protection planners do peddle that 'one quick fix' or 'magic bullet.' For instance, quite a few planners promote Nevada corporations as 'everybody's' asset protection answer. Others sell only international trusts or limited partnerships. However, these entities are only one of many possible firewalls. That's all they are. But are they *your* right firewall. Your planner must offer you the entire range of protective firewalls because any one firewall is only one more tool in the planner's toolbox. No one firewall is *everybody's* lawsuit-proofing answer. A good planner adeptly uses *every* possible protective tool.

For example, you want a planner with expertise in both international and domestic (U.S.-based) protective strategies because if you have a high net worth you'll probably need *both* domestic and international planning. Your planner must skillfully provide both. Yet, few planners have this dual expertise. The point is to choose a planner who can give you the complete arsenal of protective tools. Anything less reduces your options and protection. It's common sense. Would you go to a physician who prescribes the same medication to every patient?

Nor is it simple to customize your one *best* plan. Your planner must consider many factors: 1) your state laws, 2) the nature and value of the assets to be protected, 3) the liability (if any) to be protected against, 4) whether you need preventative or crisis planning, 5) your financial (estate planning, investment, and tax) situation, 6) the strategies you'll be most comfortable with, 7) costs, and 8) your personal situation (age, marital status, etc.). And there are other issues and considerations. Only when we expertly blend these many considerations do we arrive at your best plan; but it's only your best plan at that given point in time and against a given danger – if one exists. Customization is the essence of good planning. 'Cookie cutter' planning is bad planning.

If we are unsure whether a particular firewall will succeed in blocking a creditor, can we add firewalls?

Absolutely, and we usually do. Your asset protection plan may need only one firewall to well-shield an asset or it may require several. No matter how strong a particular firewall may be, there's some possibility that it can fail. That's why we 'layer' or use multiple firewalls. It is our 'belt and suspenders' approach to asset protection. If one firewall fails; another stands. And we impose still more firewalls should they become necessary. The challenge is to know *which* firewalls to use in a particular case, and *when* to add more firewalls. We want at least two firewalls to build a more solid plan.

Asset protection plans often evolve in stages. For instance, you may start with a *preventative* plan and advance to a *crisis* plan. Normally we add firewalls only *if* and *when* they become necessary. If you protect yourself *before* you incur a liability, you should need only one good basic level of protection using one, or possibly two, firewalls. This won't necessarily be your final plan if you're sued because your crisis plan may need additional firewalls for maximum protection against *that* particular threat. Your goal is always to be as judgment-proof as possible when you walk into the courtroom. Of course, a crisis plan is usually more costly and complex than a basic plan and that's why we usually layer firewalls only *after* a legal threat arises. Until then, we can't foresee which firewalls would give you the best protection because this greatly depends upon the amount and nature of the claim, as well as how far the creditor is likely to go to pursue your assets. So we start with a cost-effective, simple plan. After all, you may never get sued. Nor is every lawsuit wealth-threatening. So we add firewalls only as a serious threat advances. Why overbuild your plan prematurely? This forfeits flexibility and may needlessly add cost. Inevitably, your plan must give you safety, yet no plan is guaranteed. Nevertheless, multiple or combined firewalls exponentially strengthens your plan. For example, we frequently combine or layer limited partnerships with international trusts, international LLCs and international self-protected investments to create one integrated, formidable four-layer firewall barrier. But you can take advantage of countless layering possibilities to create a *'defense-in-depth'*.

Defense-in-depth sounds sensible, but isn't it also sound to title your assets to separate entities?

Absolutely. Diversification too is an important strategy. Deploying your assets into different protective 'baskets' is common sense and sound planning. Why keep all your eggs in one basket? Your goal is to force a creditor to pursue your assets dispersed in different ways, protected through different entities, and located in different jurisdictions. Should the creditor recover assets from 'one basket', the wealth sheltered in your other 'baskets' remains safe. Diversification is particularly important to protect significant wealth. For example, you would want to deploy a multi-million dollar portfolio in several protective 'baskets' – and they may be quite dissimilar. We oftentimes combine layering or 'defense-in-depth' with diversification to produce the strongest plan.

Are different plans necessary to protect against different financial dangers?

Certainly. No one plan is equally effective against *every* claim. Asset protection is much like football. The best defensive positioning in any given case is the one that can most effectively block a particular offensive line. Likewise, to protect assets against a routine civil lawsuit would probably require a far different strategy than one we would use to protect their assets against a divorce. First and foremost, your plan must effectively protect you against any known and imminent threats, or the danger that may prompt you to seek protection in the first place. Yet, you can't always foresee trouble. A preventative plan gives you a foundation or *basic* protection. We then add firewalls to effectively blockade specific threats as they appear. You can modify a flexible plan to meet each situation. You must also understand your plan's limitations and consult your advisor whenever you face a new threat. A more flexible plan also accommodates your personal lifestyle changes. Moreover, newer, more effective asset protection strategies and opportunities should also encourage you to periodically upgrade your plan. And once a particular legal threat ends you may want to partially dismantle your plan and eliminate excessive 'firewalls' that are too costly to maintain and unnecessary against future claimants. *Great* plans are 'modular' in that you can speedily add, delete or change firewalls. Our objective is to create a modular plan.

It sounds like most asset protection plans are complicated. True?

Some are, but most are surprisingly simple. Nor is a complex plan always the best plan. Simplicity is often better. We think that over-planning is a chronic planning error. Yes, you may want several firewalls to shelter yourself against a particular creditor, but you sometimes get improved protection with a less complex plan and with fewer firewalls. You'll certainly save legal fees. As importantly, you and your other advisors will better understand the simpler plan. A simpler plan is also less likely to fall into disuse. That's another reason we prefer to start with a basic plan and 'layer' the plan with more firewalls on an 'as needed' basis. Once the legal problem ends, we simplify the plan.

You have many simple ways to protect your assets. For example, you might convert non-exempt assets into exempt assets. Or you can debt-shield or encumber your assets. In some states, you might safely title your assets as tenants-by-the-entirety if you're married. You can implement other highly-effective, yet simple strategies at minimum or no cost. Most importantly, you'll more fully understand a simple plan. Whether your plan is simple or complex, your advisor must fully explain your plan and how each component fits. If *you* don't fully understand your plan, it's either too complex or your advisor has poorly explained it. Never trade safety for simplicity, but choose simplicity when a more complex plan won't give you sufficiently greater protection to balance its cost.

How can I design a less costly plan?

Cost is always an important consideration. We are sensitive to this when we design our asset protection plans. Asset protection is a great 'investment,' but it still must be cost effective. So economy and simplicity go hand-in-hand. You don't want to spend more than necessary for good protection, but you also don't want false economy and a faulty plan. That's why we seek good, low cost alternatives to more expensive structures and strategies. For example, the international LLC may, in some instances, provide equal or even superior protection to the international trust at a fraction of the cost. And as we say, a number of judgment-proofing techniques (exemptions, tenancy-by-the-entireties, etc.) cost little or nothing.

Cost is a function of both which entities and strategies you use for your plan, and of course, who you choose as your planner. However, you can't accurately 'comparison shop' planners. For example, an international incorporation service may set up an international company at less cost than an American attorney, but would the two entities have the same protective features? Is the international incorporation service merely forming an entity or also providing legal advice about how to use the entity, or even deciding whether this is your *right* entity? What does this international provider know about asset protection? And will the international provider assume responsibility for protecting your wealth? You can't compare apples and oranges. Still, most families can protect their wealth for less than they might imagine. It's indeed a small investment when your goal is peace of mind and financial security.

Would a good asset protection plan also help me avoid liabilities?

Yes. A good asset protection plan must do more than protect your assets from lawsuits. It should also *limit* your liability. You can, and must, insulate yourself personally from business and other foreseeable liabilities. Your goal is to limit creditors to the fewest assets possible. When you title your assets to different protective entities, any one lawsuit will jeopardize the fewest assets possible. For instance, a plan to shelter a business owner's personal assets is incomplete unless we also limit the creditors of the client's business to the assets of that one business. Good protection both minimizes liability and lawsuit-proofs wealth.

Is it necessary for a client to lose control over their assets to protect them?

Not usually. For instance, limited partnerships and limited liability companies allow you to retain complete control over your assets, and these entities well-protect assets. As another example, you may directly own exempt assets or title your assets with your spouse as tenants-by-the-entirety. Even when we use trusts for wealth protection, we have control retention techniques to relieve our client's fears about entrusting their assets to a trustee. There are many ways to safeguard assets entrusted to others. You expand your planning options once you fully understand these control retention techniques. How much control you can maintain over your assets must, in each instance, be determined by your advisor and ultimately the answer depends on the nature of the plan and the tools we use, and sometimes you must surrender control over your assets to a professional trustee to safeguard your assets. But isn't this preferable to losing your assets to your creditors?

Are there counter-offensive strategies that one can use to discourage lawsuits?

We follow the axiom – "The best defense is a good offense." This is no less true when it comes to asset protection. We use a number of strategies to impose liability against a creditor. For instance, we may force a creditor who obtains a charging order against a limited partnership or LLC interest to pay the income taxes on the debtor's income from the entity. Or a creditor who sues your international LLC or international trust may be required to pay a hefty bond to cover your legal fees. We can impose other liabilities on a pursuing creditor. Porcupines use quills and we add 'quills' to our asset protection plans. We want to give the creditor a 'downside' when chasing wealth. A creditor uncertain about what they might eventually recover must be very certain about what they can *lose* through litigation. The best quill of course, is to force your creditor to spend a fortune in legal fees to even *attempt* seizure of your assets.

What are the differences between a good and great asset protection plan?

Great lawsuit protection doesn't just happen. First and foremost, if you are to most effectively block litigants and creditors from claiming your assets, you should protect yourself *before* trouble strikes. You also need the *right* strategies and tools for your particular situation. A *good* plan may safe keep your assets yet few *good* plans are *great* plans. A *great* plan gives you additional benefits. The plan is ideal for *you*. We have reviewed thousands of asset protection plans and an endless variety of strategies and techniques. While no two planners are likely to propose precisely the same plan; nevertheless, we found that many 'good' plans could easily have been *great* plans with a bit more thought. A great plan provides *more* protection and benefits with less cost and complexity. And to create that great plan, your planner must fully understand your other financial and personal goals and, most importantly, have the skill and caring to achieve those diverse goals within the context of providing sound protection.

How frequently should I update my asset protection plan?

Asset protection – like estate planning – must be continuous. You may hurriedly protect yourself if you are sued, but letting your plan fall into disuse once the threat passes can be costly. You must change your asset protection plan as your finances, obligations and personal situation changes. Laws and strategies also change, and each necessitates changing your asset protection plan. You should review your plan at least annually and more frequently if you have a major change to your finances or personal affairs. It takes time, cost and effort to enjoy lifelong protection, but that's a small price. If you allow your protection to erode because it's no longer important to you, you again become vulnerable.

What are the most common planning errors to avoid?

With asset protection planning there are many things that one can do wrong. The three biggest blunders are those mistakes that can breach your protection or get you into trouble. You'll want to particularly avoid: 1) fraudulent transfers; 2) titling your assets to a 'straw', and 3) concealing your assets. But there are many other errors one can make.

What is a fraudulent transfer?

Every state has fraudulent transfer laws. Some call it the *Uniform Fraudulent Conveyance Act (UFCA),* and others the *Uniform Fraudulent Transfer Act (UFTA).* *Fraudulent transfers* or *fraudulent conveyances* laws can be interchangeably discussed here since they are so similar. The fraudulent transfer laws essentially let a judgment creditor unwind transfers previously made by a debtor so that the fraudulently transferred property can be claimed by the creditor. In other words, given certain circumstances, courts invalidate and revoke prior sales, gifts or other transfers. Whatever assets the debtor sold or gave away for less than fair value are then re-transferred to the judgment creditor. Fraudulent transfers then partially or totally destroy your protection.

For effective protection, you must *safely* title your wealth. That's the only way to keep your wealth *beyond* the reach of your creditors. Judgment creditors trying to seize a debtor's wealth often use the fraudulent transfer laws to seize assets the debtor previously transferred. The fraudulent transfer may be to a spouse, other relative, friend, corporation, partnership, trust or anyone else. Whether the creditor can succeed on their fraudulent transfer claim chiefly depends on whether the creditor can convince the court that the transfer was simply a last-ditch effort to defraud the creditor.

What must a creditor prove to win a fraudulent transfer case?

There are two types of fraudulent transfers: 1) Fraud in fact, or *actual fraud,* and 2) Fraud in law, or *constructive fraud.* Actual fraud is when you actually *intended* to hinder, delay or defraud your creditor. This, of course, is usually difficult to prove because the creditor must prove your state of mind – unless you admit to fraudulent intent. However, courts can infer fraudulent intent from *badges of fraud* such as transfers to close family members or friends, secretive transfers, transfers for less than fair value, situations when the debtor continued to use or possess the property after the transfer, concealing assets, transfers made after the debtor incurred a large debt or anticipated a lawsuit, and transfers that rendered the debtor unable to pay the debt. It's important to understand that a fraudulent transfer is not the same as fraud. Fraudulent transfers should more appropriately be called 'voidable transfers'.

What if I transferred my assets but didn't actually intend to defraud my creditor?

Since actual fraud cases are difficult for creditors to prove, creditors more often claim *constructive fraud.* Constructive fraud is a gift or sale of property for less than fair value (or *fair consideration*), made in the face of a known or probable liability and which leaves the debtor insolvent. A transfer can be constructively fraudulent, even if you act innocently and without actual intent to hinder your creditors, but a creditor challenging your transfer must still prove each of these three elements.

When is a transfer for less than fair value?

One obvious situation is when the debtor merely gifts his assets. However, proving a sale was made for less than fair value can sometimes be difficult to prove. Courts define 'fair' consideration subjectively. 'Fair' consideration is the price for which a reasonably prudent seller would sell his property in a commercially reasonable manner. 'Fair value' depends largely on the type of property. For example, public stocks or bonds have an ascertainable fair value and a debtor who transfers public shares for less than its daily quoted price would create a fraudulent transfer equal to the difference in value. Conversely, real estate sold for 70 percent of appraised value has been held to satisfy the fair value test. Other difficult-to-value items include jewelry and the closely-owned business. Courts must then consider the relevant facts to determine 'reasonable value'.

What do you mean by a transfer after you incur a 'present liability'?

If you sell an asset for less than its fair value, the creditor must secondly show that the transfer occurred after you had the liability. Once you have a *present* liability, you cannot safely transfer your assets for less than fair value. No less safe are assets that you transfer when you have a future, foreseeable or *probable liability*. But you can safely transfer your assets to protect them against a future *possible liability*. How do we differentiate a *probable* from a *possible liability?* The courts consider the facts of each case. When did the act occur that created the liability? When did the debtor first learn of the liability? When was the transfer? Courts conclude differently on whether a liability was *probable* or *possible*.

A *'present* liability' exists from the moment you have a creditor (incurred a liability). Later asset transfers can be challenged. For example, if you sign a lease today and gift your assets tomorrow, your landlord can recover your gifted assets if you later default on your lease. You didn't have to be in default on your lease for your transfer to be fraudulent. It's also immaterial whether you were yet sued. The critical date is when did the liability arise – not the date of default or when the lawsuit was filed.

It seems that the fraudulent transfer laws are somewhat subjective. How can you be certain a transfer isn't fraudulent?

Frequently you can't. When you review these three elements of a constructive fraudulent transfer, you still have hundreds of unanswered questions. For instance, is it fraudulent to exchange non-exempt assets for exempt (protected) assets of equal value? What if you transfer your assets at the time you have a *foreseeable* creditor (i.e. you expect to sign a lease)? We can go on. The fraudulent transfer laws are complex, murky, and there can be gray areas of uncertainty. Many transfers are neither clearly fraudulent nor conclusively non-fraudulent. A seasoned asset protection specialist can perhaps best understand the complexities and apply the nuances of these laws to best predict whether a court is likely to unwind a transfer.

Does this suggest that it's too late to protect my assets once I am sued or have a potential liability?

Not necessarily. No law obligates a lawsuit defendant to hold his assets for the benefit of his creditors, despite common belief to the contrary. In fact, Supreme Court Justice Antonin Scalia, in one celebrated case, announced, "A creditor has no cognizable interest in the assets of a debtor prior to obtaining a judgment. Anyone can transfer their assets all day long until the sheriff shows up with a Writ of Execution pursuant to a court order."

Also contrary to popular misconception, a fraudulent transfer *isn't* a crime. It's a civil remedy. It divides *irreversible* transfers from transfers that can later be reversed by the courts. With a fraudulent transfer, the transferor and transferee don't commit a crime. And frequently, a defendant's attorney can successfully argue that the transfer wasn't fraudulent. However, even if the defendant loses, the court remedy is only to unwind the transfer.

31

The essence of fraudulent transfer law was well-stated in one Florida Supreme Court case: "A fraudulent conveyance action is simply another creditor remedy. It is either an action by a creditor against a transferee directed against a particular transaction which, if declared fraudulent, is set aside, thus leaving the creditor free to pursue the asset, or it is an action against a transferee who has received an asset by means of a fraudulent conveyance and should be required to either return the asset or pay for the asset. A fraudulent conveyance action is *not* an action against a debtor for failure to pay an amount owing from a prior judgment and does not warrant an *additional* judgment against the same debtor because of the fraudulent conveyance."

Clearly, it's not too late to take defensive measures once you are sued – though you have fewer options than had you planned beforehand. Still, even the most dire of situations has its solutions. Again, to quote the Supreme Court, "A debtor [who is sued] need not be like a deer frozen in the headlights of an onrushing auto. The debtor still has it within his rights the opportunity to attempt to put his wealth beyond harm's way."

The safest path, of course, is to protect yourself *before* you encounter problems. You then have more planning options and less risk that your transfer will later be challenged. Still, many clients in litigation are advised by their attorney that it's too late to protect their assets because a lawsuit has begun or is threatened. This is poor advice. It makes no more sense than a doctor advising a patient that it's too late to try to save herself because she has already contracted a disease. Yes, you have fewer wealth-saving alternatives once you have a claim against you, and yes, you need more creative and complex planning to safely shelter your assets – but you *do* have options.

When is the best time to protect your assets?

What should be obvious from our conversation so far is that the best time to protect yourself is before a creditor threat is foreseeable. You should always protect yourself:

- Well before your marriage turns sour and heads for divorce. Preferably, if you wish to do specific pre-marital/pre-divorce planning, and a pre-nuptial agreement is not an option, then set up your program before you get married. Plan at least one year before you divorce.
- Before someone threatens you with a lawsuit.
- Before your business starts going under.

In other words, because we often can't foresee creditor threats before they materialize, a protective plan is best implemented before these threats occur. In sum, you should set up an asset protection plan as soon as possible!

Can we protect you after a threat to your wealth arises? Except in some circumstances, the answer is usually yes. But your asset protection program will definitely be stronger if it's set up well before your wealth becomes threatened. Furthermore, you may have to take more complex and expensive steps to protect your assets after your problems appear. Our plans may then include international planning with exclusively international managers, or even something as radical, however pleasant, as moving to Florida to buy a homestead property which is protected against creditors, even if the home purchase is a fraudulent transfer.

Generally speaking, it's too late to try to protect yourself once you have a judgment against you, unless you arrange to pay the judgment and you follow through with that arrangement and are only planning to safeguard your assets against future creditors. Asset protection planning to thwart collection attempts post-judgment may result in you and your asset protection planner being fined and you can then be worse off than if you planned.

Can a creditor seize my assets or prevent me from transferring my assets before they have a judgment?

Generally not. Litigants, who have yet to win a judgment, ordinarily *cannot* commence a fraudulent transfer claim or freeze your assets. This is a remedy for *judgment creditors*. Nor can a *pre-judgment creditor* usually attach assets or restrain a defendant's rights to transfer his assets – even if the planned transfer appears fraudulent. The plaintiff's remedy is to recover the asset as fraudulently transferred *after* the creditor wins his case. But there are exceptions when a court does allow a freeze order or attachment of a defendant's assets before the lawsuit is commenced. That's why delay in seeking protection is *always* dangerous.

What is the statute of limitations for a creditor to recover fraudulently transferred assets?

In most states a fraudulent transfer lawsuit must be filed within four years from the date of the transfer or one year after the transfer could have been reasonably discovered by the creditor. In these instances, a fraudulently transferred asset is never completely safe from recovery because a creditor can argue they only recently discovered a transfer which may have happened years earlier. The creditor would then have one additional year to set aside the transfer. Other states impose a strict five-year statute of limitations and disallow later claims regardless of when the creditor discovered the transfer.

How can one reduce their chances of a fraudulent transfer claim?

Use common sense. Avoid the badges of fraud. Don't invite suspicion and inquiry. Your transfers must pass a 'sniff' test. First, *protect yourself before you have a liability*. There's no fraudulent transfer if you transfer your assets *before* you incur the liability. That's the reason for the axiom to judgment-proof yourself *before* you have financial or legal problems. Your safest strategy is to be liability-free when you protect your assets. If you still have fraudulent transfer concerns, *make small incremental transfers, which* will attract less notice than sudden transfers of more significant assets. Also, *avoid insider transactions.* Transfers to family members, friends or close business associates are always suspicious. Use non-family members as trustees, corporate officers or fiduciaries for any entities receiving your assets. Your transfer should not have the obvious goal of defrauding a present creditor. It might better appear that you were engaged in estate planning. Finally, *carefully document what you receive for your property.* Can you prove you were adequately paid in cash, services or other consideration? *Verify the value of your property* to show fair consideration. For example, get your home appraised if you sell it to a friend or relative. If you sell assets for an unreasonably low price, document defects or other reasons to justify its low price.

It seems that the first step to defensive planning is to get your assets out of your own name. Correct?

We agree. Unless your assets are exempt, title them to a protective entity. As long as the entity itself is not a debtor, then a subsequent transfer by that entity will not be considered fraudulent under the UFTA. Accordingly, when creditor threat arises, you can then reinforce the entity or transfer the asset to a new entity, with less fraudulent transfer concerns because the UFTA only considers transfers the debtor makes as being fraudulent. Furthermore, restructuring an entity so that a creditor of the entity's owner cannot reach the entity's assets for its owner's debts usually does not involve a transfer, and is therefore not considered to be a fraudulent transfer in most states. Even if it is, as long as the entity is not a debtor, then a transfer from the non-debtor entity to another entity is usually not considered fraudulent under fraudulent transfer law.

For protection why can't I just title my assets to someone else so they can't be claimed by my creditors?

Using 'straw men' is always poor planning. Its pitfalls are obvious. First is the fraudulent conveyance pitfall. Gifting your assets to a friend or relative *after* you're sued with the tacit understanding that they'll later return your assets seldom works. Even if you title your assets to a 'straw' *before* you have creditors, how do you know that your 'straw' is safer from lawsuits than you? Nominee 'straws' have their own marital problems, tax troubles, creditors and lawsuits. Your straw can easily lose *your*

35

assets to *their* creditors. You also incur a gift tax when you transfer assets to someone other than your spouse. And your nominee straw incurs a gift tax when he re-transfers your assets to you. The third problem is that you can't be certain that your nominee will return your assets. Not every straw or nominee is trustworthy. Finally, a 'straw' deal is asset concealment. This may be a crime in your situation. It certainly would be if you file bankruptcy or you commit perjury to disguise the nature of your transaction.

What about titling marital assets to my spouse who has less liability exposure?

Having a less liability-prone spouse own all the marital assets has fewer drawbacks. And sometimes it is sensible to title the family assets to the less vulnerable spouse. But this too raises problems. You may title your million dollar home or other assets to your spouse for protection on the belief that your spouse *won't* get sued, but how do you really know this? This arrangement also has estate planning disadvantages. When marital assets are titled to *both* spouses, the spouses can more advantageously plan their estates because each can use credit shelter trusts to maximize their death tax credits. When the assets are titled to only one spouse, only that spouse can claim his or her estate tax exemption. The remainder of your spouse's estate will be taxed. This can cost your heirs a considerable estate tax. Assets titled to only one spouse forces a lopsided estate plan, and you lose tax planning options.

Nor are assets titled to one spouse necessarily safe from the debtor spouse's creditors. Even if the liability arose *after* the debtor's assets were titled to the 'safe' spouse, a creditor might successfully argue that the debtor-spouse has an equitable or beneficial interest in at least part of the property under a constructive or resulting trust theory; namely, that the spouse holding title is a trustee for the debtor-spouse. This argument is particularly likely to succeed when the debtor-spouse's funds purchased the property or paid the mortgage, maintenance or property upkeep. When the money invested in the asset came from the debtor-spouse, the property is not truly the property of the *other* spouse. If a debtor-spouse's assets are traceable to property, the defendant's spouse's creditors can claim that property. You don't want to gamble on further litigation over these sloppy issues. The best plan is free of these possible challenges. Only in a few cases do we suggest titling all the marital assets to one spouse.

What are the dangers of simply hiding my assets – perhaps in some international jurisdiction – and not revealing these assets to my creditor?

That's a common mistake. One must never confuse secrecy or concealing assets with asset protection, though to discourage lawsuits, financial privacy can sometimes be helpful. A judgment creditor can compel you to disclose your finances under oath. You can't then rely on secrecy. Once under oath you must truthfully disclose your assets. It's perjury to lie to conceal your assets. You want honest protection. With a good plan you can fully disclose your assets, confident that they'll stay creditor-proof. A judgment creditor is entitled to full and honest answers about your present and past assets.

How easily can creditors find undisclosed assets?

A judgment creditor has many ways to make you disclose your finances. Depositions, interrogatories and requests to produce documents are all options. Your creditors can also subpoena your records and information from third parties. A judgment creditor searching for your assets can check loan and credit applications, bank records, tax returns, court cases (i.e. prior divorces disclose assets) and insurance policies. The paper trail is revealing. Computers make everyone's financial affairs an open book.

Because the ways to gain financial secrecy are so sophisticated, judgment creditors and prospective litigants hire professional asset search firms to locate hidden assets – even whether the prospective defendant has enough assets to make a lawsuit worthwhile. Assume your creditor can accurately profile you. Forensic accounting firms trace millions in wealth deviously and secretively deployed. So it's best to avoid the 'hide the assets' game. It's foolhardy. Your creditor will probably find your assets.

When is it too late to protect my assets?

Before we discuss when you should not do asset protection, we should examine when asset protection planning is safe. As long as the asset protection does not involve fraud or blatant illegal acts it is safest to do asset protection while the creditor seas are calm and the debtor is solvent. In doing so, even a flawed asset protection program may have a fighting chance of holding up when challenged. Remember, however, that solid asset protection has a much higher chance of surviving scrutiny than flawed planning.

Once a creditor threat has arisen, asset protection may still be done, although our available options are now somewhat diminished. Nonetheless, the U.S. Supreme Court case *Grupo Mexican v. Alliance Bond Fund* states, "[we] follow the well-established general rule that a judgment establishing the debt was necessary before a court of equity would interfere with the debtor's use of the property." Another court even noted that an attorney who represents a client under creditor attack should "protect [the client] from the claims of creditors, to the fullest permissible extent." This obviously gives us some wiggle room, and we believe an attorney has an *obligation* to recommend asset protection for his client in certain situations; however, the key phrase is that we must do our planning "to the fullest *permissible* extent". This means planning while under creditor duress should only be done while fully considering the UFTA. Furthermore, there are several pitfalls that should be avoided at all costs.

This brings us finally to circumstances where asset protection should not be done. Planning done in these instances can not only cause a program to fail, but could result in additional fines and penalties against the debtor, the planner, and possibly professional discipline against the debtor's attorney. Such circumstances can be broken down into four categories, and include; 1) planning against a creditor who has a direct interest in the property; 2) planning against a post-judgment creditor; 3) planning that involves dishonesty, misrepresentation, or committing a fraud against the court; and 4) planning that is a blatant and egregious fraudulent transfer under the UFTA.

A responsible attorney won't get involved in asset protection planning for a client under any of these circumstances.

It seems there are as many things that one can do wrong in asset protection planning as they can do right. Is that so?

Unquestionably. Most errors are a matter of extreme. There are too many firewalls or too few. Or the wrong firewalls are used. Or there are negative tax consequences that were not considered. Or the plan doesn't fit with the client's estate plan. A good part of our work is to reconstruct a client's plan. But don't get us wrong. We also see many creative, well-designed plans. But too often the present plan needs adjustment – if the client has a plan at all which is in itself unusual.

What is the #1 planning error?

Planning too late. It comes back to that one word – procrastination. But why should that be surprising. Who really thinks about protecting their wealth until they're in jeopardy of losing it? That's when they begin to 'sweat'. And, typically, that's when they call us. But think about it from a different viewpoint. Only one out of five adult Americans have even a simple will, and what is more certain than death? It is little wonder so few people think about asset protection until they are sued.

Americans are not necessarily risk-takers; we just don't always put things in perspective. For example, fifty million new lawsuits will be filed this year, yet there will be only five million injuries and deaths from car accidents. You are then ten times more likely to get sued than to injure or kill someone in a car accident. However, you wouldn't go without car insurance. You would be ten times as foolish to ignore lawsuit protection. And the number of new civil lawsuits this year will be nearly eighty times the number of residential fires. You probably have insurance to protect your home against fire, but what simple steps have you taken to safeguard your home from lawsuits and creditors? It's all logic, but that's not how most people think about these things. And it's unfortunate because we have seen so many people and families needlessly lose everything they have worked a lifetime to accumulate. It's sad.

3

Asset

Protection

Tools

Thank you for your overview of the planning fundamentals. Now let's discuss some of the specific tools or 'firewalls' that you use for asset protection. Is one better than another?

Not necessarily. Each tool or firewall has its place and purpose. And firewalls can also be combined to give stronger protection in a given case. Once you more fully understand how each firewall works, you better understand how to best develop your plan. More importantly, you'll understand how and why your plan will work, and how each firewall will help insulate your assets.

You mention owning exempt assets as the first protective strategy. Which assets are exempt from creditor seizure?

Exemption planning is the process of reorganizing one's wealth so that much of it is protected (or 'exempt') by law from creditor attachment, even though it is still owned by that individual. There are some assets that are exempt under federal law, but most exemptions come from state law. Then there are bankruptcy exemptions, which may involve federal and/or state exemptions, and which apply only in bankruptcy. State protected assets vary greatly from state to state as do the extent to which these assets are protected. However, there are general categories of exempt assets set by both the federal government and each state. Other assets are exempt under bankruptcy law. Assets that are commonly exempt include the home equity, wages, pensions and retirement accounts, profit sharing plans, annuities and insurance, tools of the trade, certain household items, burial plots, jewelry and other personal possessions.

Since the exemption laws do vary between states, you must check your own state laws to see which assets are specifically exempt in your state. You have other exemptions if you file bankruptcy. There are also various conditions and restrictions to qualify for these exemptions. You'll want to review them with your asset protection and/or bankruptcy attorneys so you gain the *maximum* exemption protection.

At first glance, you would think exemption planning is simple. After all, if the law says an asset is exempt, then it's exempt. That's not always so. There are always exceptions, caveats, and conditions to the exemption laws. Knowing when an 'exempt' asset is really exempt from a certain creditor and when it is not is what you would expect the asset protection planners to know.

With our own clients, we mostly discuss exemption planning in a non-bankruptcy context. However, when one files for bankruptcy the exemption rules change considerably. Therefore, with exemption planning one must consider the likelihood of an individual declaring bankruptcy in the future. Even if bankruptcy is unlikely, one must plan for the contingency that it could happen. For example, an individual could be involuntarily petitioned into bankruptcy (Chapters 7 or 11) by three or more creditors if their aggregate claim exceeds $12,300, or even by one creditor if the debtor has fewer than 12 creditors, and the creditor filing the petition has claims exceeding, in the aggregate, $12,300.

The law of the state where one resides determines whether one may use state exemptions only, or whether one may choose between state or federal exemptions when they are in bankruptcy. If a state allows a choice of federal or state, then one may choose one set of exemptions – but not both. The federal exemption amount, in bankruptcy, may be doubled for a married couple, although this may or may not be the case with the state exemptions. Note that moving to a more exemption-friendly state before one files bankruptcy only works if the move is made at least 730 days (about 2 years) before filing.

As we can see from our discussion, there are some particular problems with exemption and pre-bankruptcy planning. These concerns mostly arise in three areas. The first involves the shifting of exemption rules from a non-bankruptcy to a bankruptcy scenario. The second problem involves a shift in rules, in both non-bankruptcy and bankruptcy scenarios, when the individual moves to another state. The third problem involves creditors, such as the IRS or another state, which may be able to ignore the exemption laws. Because it's impossible to say for sure that an individual will never declare bankruptcy, or that they'll always live in one state, or that they'll never have IRS or other government agency problems, with the exception of a few asset classes (such as ERISA-governed plans that will not enter payout status for many years) we must structure an exemption plan sufficiently flexible to changes due to an individual's change in circumstances.

Once I'm sued can I then convert my non-exempt assets into exempt assets?

It may then be too late. Many courts consider this a fraudulent transfer. You may attempt it, but it's not wise to rely on this one strategy alone if you already have a liability. Many states also have anti-conversion statutes that deny the exemption to certain exempt assets purchased after you have a liability.

Where can I find the list of federal and state exemptions?

Check our website www.AssetProtectionAttorneys.com.

How significant a role does exemption planning play in asset protection?

That answer mostly depends on the debtor's state laws. Several states – most notably Florida and Texas – are exceptionally debtor oriented. They exempt, or creditor proof, a wide range of assets. That's why a large number of debtors relocate to Florida. It is not so much to enjoy their favorable weather, as it is to take advantage of their generous exemption laws. For instance, Florida protects the entire value of your home, IRAs, life insurance and annuities, and wages. Many of our Florida clients need little or nothing more in terms of additional protection. The state exemption laws cover all – or most – of their assets. Texas is an equally debtor friendly state. On the other hand, a number of states are creditor friendly with narrow exemption laws. New Jersey is an example where relatively few assets are self-protected.

You suggest co-ownership as another way to gain protection. What is co-ownership planning and how do co-ownerships work?

One form of protective co-ownership is tenancy-by-the-entirety (TBE). Twenty-five states, at least to some extent, protect assets owned by spouses as T/E against the creditors of only one spouse. Some T/E states limit their protection only to the family residence and other states extend their protection to other real estate, and still other states extend their protection to any assets, including stocks, bonds, personal property, and so forth that are titled as tenants-by-the-entirety.

Co-ownership planning is the concurrent ownership of property by two or more people. The most common co-ownerships involve assets owned between a husband and wife. When we refer to co-ownerships, we do not usually mean the co-ownership of business entities by multiple individuals (unless an undivided interest is held jointly or as tenants-by-the-entirety), nor do we refer to multiple beneficial interests in a trust.

There are four types of co-ownerships namely; 1) tenancy-in-common (TIC); 2) joint tenants with right of survivorship (JTWROS); JTWROS is often

44

referred to simply as 'joint tenants' ownership; 3) tenants-by-the-entirety (TBE); and 4) community property.

It's important to understand the distinguishing features of each. Many folks don't understand the consequences of co-owning assets with others.

You say that if spouses hold property as tenancy-by-the-entirety it may provide protection for the asset. Can you expand upon this?

Certainly. Of the four types of co-ownership, only tenancy-by-the-entirety (TBE) may provide meaningful asset protection. Tenancy-by-the-entirety is a special type of co-ownership only available to a husband and wife. Tenancy-by-the-entirety ownership must also meet the requirements of joint tenancy in order to be valid. And if a couple divorces, then ownership will be held as tenants-in-common or as joint tenants rather than as tenants-by-the-entirety. Tenancy-by-the-entirety offers right of survivorship benefits (as does joint tenancy), but it may also protect the asset in certain states, provided only one spouse comes under creditor attack. This is because, in most states, tenancy-by-the-entirety property may not be transferred or otherwise alienated without the other spouse's consent. Furthermore, neither spouse owns a fractional share in the property. Rather, each spouse claims an entire ownership interest in the property, but such ownership rights is subject to the other spouse maintaining their property rights as well. Because their respective ownership interests are not divisible and may not be transferred without the other spouse's consent, most Tenancy-by-the-entirety states do not allow a creditor of only one spouse to attach tenancy-by-the-entirety property without the consent of both spouses.

Unfortunately, tenancy-by-the-entirety ownership is not available in all states. And in those states where it is available, it may not be allowed for all assets. Some states prohibit tenancy-by-the-entirety ownership either by case or statutory law, and in other states it is unclear whether tenancy-by-the-entirety ownership is allowed. One should still consult the statutory and case law of his or her particular state, as there are further differences in tenancy-by-the-entirety laws. For example, a few states restrict tenancy-by-the-entirety ownership only to primary residences.

Alaska, Hawaii, Tennessee and Vermont specifically allow rental real estate to be held in tenancy-by-the-entirety, yet other states may allow it by case law.

There are many cases where tenancy-by-the-entirety ownership has successfully shielded assets. Nonetheless, we usually conclude that this form of ownership cannot be relied upon as an impenetrable creditor defense. On the upside, it's very easy to title assets as tenants-by-the-entirety between a husband and wife in those states that allow it, and in those states, it is a great way to add an extra layer of protection.

For example, in a state that recognizes tenancy-by-the-entirety ownership, it may be a good idea to so title the ownership of business entities as tenancy-by-the-entirety. Nonetheless, merely saying an asset is held in the tenancy-by-the-entirety is not sufficient. The title documents to the asset should expressly state that the asset is held as tenants-by-the-entirety.

Can other forms of co-ownership protect your assets?

Not generally. For example, two or more parties may own property as tenants-in-common, yet that's a dangerous form of ownership because each co-owner's interest is vulnerable to his or her creditors. As importantly, these co-owners are both personally liable for any liability created by the asset. The same is true with property jointly owned with right of survivorship (JTWROS). Families and spouses often use this form of ownership to avoid probate, but it presents the same problems as tenancy-in-common. It's far safer to co-own assets through a protective entity – such as a limited partnership or LLC – than as tenants-in-common or JTWROS, because these entities limit your personal liability. Moreover, your ownership interest in these entities would also be protected from your personal creditors. Direct co-ownerships other than as tenants-by-the-entirety is almost always a mistake.

What are the dangers of owning assets as tenants-in-common?

Each co-owner in a tenancy-in-common or *tenant-in-common* own a divided fractional share of the property. This creates serious lawsuit dangers and, reciprocally, no creditor protection. There are many examples to illustrate the risks of tenants-in-common. For instance, if you and your friend John are tenants-in-common and own an apartment building, each of you can sell, gift, or mortgage your half interest in the building without the consent of the other. You are thus essentially 'partners' in the business of renting apartments, collecting rents, maintaining the premises, etc., and the building provides you an income. Perhaps someday you expect to sell the building for a hefty profit.

Since you and John are tenants-in-common, you each own a separate share in the building which is distinct from the interests of the other tenants-in-common. Your personal creditors cannot claim your co-owner's interest and, conversely, if John is sued for reasons unrelated to the building, John's creditors can only claim *his* half interest in the building. Your half remains safe from John's creditors. While this may seem acceptable, particularly if you see yourself as the *safe* co-owner, a tenancy-in-common can nevertheless cause problems.

One big risk is that your co-owner's creditors can force a sale of the *entire* property to satisfy your co-owner's personal debts. Since your co-tenant, John, can transfer his share of the tenancy-in-common property without your consent, John's creditor can 'step into his shoes' and similarly sell his interest. You may possibly negotiate to buy your co-owner's interest to avoid the forced sale of the entire property, but this is not always practical; you may not have the money. Should the court force the sale of the entire property, you will nevertheless lose the property, although you will recover your half share of the net proceeds from the forced sale.

Suppose John's creditors do not force the sale of the entire property but instead successfully bid for John's half interest in the property. You now have a new partner – John's creditor! It can and does happen. You can see that John's financial problems can cause you serious problems, and your problems can become John's headache. More importantly, how safe is *your* ownership interest from your own creditors when you own property as tenants-in-common? You already know the answer: If John's creditors can seize his interest, your creditors can seize *yours*.

This is why co-owning property as tenants-in-common is too risky. If you or your co-owner has financial problems, you can easily lose control of the property or you might lose significant money. Avoid this trap. We will later tell you about many better ways to co-own assets through various protective entities. If you insist upon titling assets as tenants-in-common, then make certain that your co-tenants are financially secure; otherwise you risk a forced sale, a new co-owner or lost control of your investment.

Aside from the vulnerability of your co-ownership interest, perhaps an even bigger pitfall is that tenancy-in-common *expands* your liability. If John accidentally injures somebody through his negligent management of the co-owned property, who gets sued? Both you and John, of course. Since you co-own the property, you essentially created a general partnership. Should the plaintiff win a $5 million judgment or any amount that exceeds what the property or John is personally worth – who pays? *You*, of course. As co-owners, you and John have joint and several liability for any liability that arises from co-ownership of the property. The bottom line is never to own property directly as tenants-in-common. Co-own the asset indirectly through a protective entity.

How would co-owning assets as joint tenants differ?

Joint tenancy is a particularly popular form of co-ownership. Several key features distinguish it from tenancy-in-common. One such feature is its right of survivorship. When one joint tenant dies, the jointly owned property automatically passes to the surviving joint tenant(s). Jointly owned property then passes *outside* a will, and thus avoids the expense and delay of probate. Because joint tenancy avoids probate, many financial and legal advisors recommend that their clients title their assets as joint tenancy. Unfortunately, these advisors don't always tell their clients how joint ownership can hurt them. In our view, joint tenancy is nearly always a mistake because it significantly increases lawsuit risks, frustrates sound estate planning and provides little or no lawsuit protection.

For starters, jointly owned property, whether personal property or real estate, creates the same lawsuit and creditor risks as does tenancy-in-common. In some circumstances you can have greater exposure. Generally, you also have the same lack of protection as you do with tenancy-in-common. Your personal creditors can seize only your interest in the co-owned property. You also have about the same tenancy-in-common risks. If your co-owner(s) has legal or financial problems, his creditors can claim his interest in the property and become your co-tenant. Alternatively the creditor can force a sale of the entire property to recover the debt owed by your co-owner(s).

However, joint ownership has an added twist. It puts you in a 'winner-takes-all' game. You 'gamble' that you will survive your co-owner (joint tenant). Because jointly owned property automatically passes to the surviving joint tenant(s), if the liability-free tenant dies before the debtor tenant, the entire property automatically passes to the debtor, and the entire property can then be claimed by the surviving debtor's creditors. For example, if you and John own the building as joint tenants, and you die, John's creditors could then levy or seize the entire building. Your family would have no further ownership claim to the building. Of course, the alternative outcome in this 'winner-takes-all' game is that if the safe co-owner (you) survives the debtor co-owner (John), you own the entire building free of John's creditors. This may be one advantage with joint tenancy: It is you who may win the game.

Joint tenancy also impairs good estate planning. For instance, if your estate plan is to gift your property at your death to your friends, you would normally provide for this in your will or living trust. Joint tenancy may frustrate this estate planning objective because whatever property is jointly owned instead passes automatically by rights of survivorship to your surviving joint tenant(s). This automatic transfer occurs the instant you die. Your will or living trust would be totally ineffective in disposing of any jointly owned property. Any beneficiaries that you designate in your will or trust to inherit your share of jointly owned property are effectively 'disinherited' since the property instead goes to the surviving joint tenant(s). We see this avoidable tragedy every day because many people do not understand this survivorship feature about joint ownership, nor do their advisors always inform them. And, as we say, plenty of folks have absolutely no idea how their assets are titled or its consequences. They should review these issues with their attorney.

How can we protect our assets if we live in a community property state?

There are nine community property states. Community property includes all marital assets. There are also separate assets; those acquired by either spouse through gift or inheritance, acquired before marriage, or specifically partitioned by the spouses into separate property. The community property laws don't protect marital assets from creditor claims against one spouse; however, separate property of the non-liable spouse is generally sheltered from claims against the other spouse if the debt didn't benefit both spouses. Generally, it is wisest to protect both community property and separate property through other means.

A married couple may partition and separately own assets in a community property state via a *transmutation agreement*. A transmutation agreement is a type of post-nuptial agreement wherein each spouse agrees to keep their own property separate and outside the community estate. A well-drafted transmutation agreement thus supersedes community property law. When drafting a transmutation agreement, each spouse should retain separate counsel and have full disclosure of the agreement's ramifications in order to prevent the agreement from later challenge. If one spouse is particularly vulnerable to creditor threats, a transmutation agreement allows the less vulnerable spouse to separately hold assets, which may provide some asset protection if it is done before the more vulnerable spouse has creditor problems. There are, however, some potential downsides to this solution.

The community property law of some states actually increases one's likelihood of losing marital assets to creditors. Some states allow a creditor to claim all community assets to cover the debts of either spouse. In contrast, a few states' community property laws actually provide limited protection. For example, Arizona allows a debt acquired by either spouse prior to marriage to be satisfied from community property, but only to the extent of the value of that spouse's contribution to the community that would have been such spouse's separate property if he or she were single. In contrast, an unsecured debt acquired during marriage may not be satisfied from community property. Nevada allows a spouse's separate debt to be

50

satisfied from community property, but only if the wife acquires debt because the husband didn't provide for her necessities. Such a debt can then be satisfied from any community property, or from the husband's separate property. In Texas, only tort debts, not contract debts, may be satisfied from community property, but if the debt arises from a tort, then it may be satisfied from any and all community property. The same can be said for tort debts in Washington, except they may only be satisfied from the debtor's half of community property. On the other hand, California, Louisiana, Idaho, New Mexico, and Wisconsin allow a separate debt acquired by either spouse during marriage to be satisfied out of any community property.

As you can see, each state's community property laws have important differences in the construction or interpretation. If you live in a community property state, you should review with your attorney precisely how your state laws work. Focus on what specific rights creditors have to claim both community and separate property. We necessarily speak in generalities. Your community property state may follow somewhat different rules.

It sounds as though one should seriously consider whether any co-ownership arrangement is right for them. Do you agree?

Positively. Those co-owning property seldom contemplate the potential liabilities they can incur from their co-ownership. Nor do they always consider whether their co-ownership aids or impedes the protection of the assets from their personal creditors.

Consider again the example of two business partners who title investment property in their personal names as tenants-in-common. If someone gets injured on the property, who has liability? How could these co-owners have more intelligently titled their property to reduce their personal exposure? What if one co-owner loses a lawsuit? What more could – and should – have been done to safeguard the debtor-partner's interest in the property?

Or consider an elderly mother with a middle-aged daughter. The mother wants to leave her savings account to her daughter when she dies and also wants her daughter to have access to the account in the event the mother becomes disabled. So she sets up a joint account and titles her bank account in both the names of herself

51

and her daughter as joint owners. Mom logically reasons that when she dies the money will automatically pass to her daughter avoiding probate. It sounds so sensible. But does mom realize the potential pitfalls and liabilities of a joint bank account? What if the daughter is sued or has her own creditor problems or divorces? Poof! A healthy chunk of the savings accounts would then go elsewhere. You see, people don't think much about these things.

Married couples often see co-ownership as their simplest, most natural way to title their marital property, but they too, must ask themselves the same questions: Will co-owning their assets increase their respective liability? Will they get more or less lawsuit protection? And will co-ownership help or hinder their other estate and tax planning objectives?

You indicate that corporations are another possible firewall. How does a corporation protect assets?

A corporation creates a barrier between your personal assets and the corporation's creditors. In other words, you gain 'inside-out' protection. You personally insulate yourself from the debts of the corporation. But this too has its limitations. If you own a corporation and get sued by a personal creditor, your personal creditor can claim your shares in the corporation. If you own a substantial share of the corporation the creditor can then liquidate the corporation and claim its assets. That's why we instead use limited partnerships, limited liability companies, irrevocable trusts or other protective firewalls to shelter your stock ownership in a corporation. So we rarely use corporations in our planning to protect personal assets, since the corporation offers no protective advantages over LLCs or LPs. Moreover, the corporation can impose negative tax consequences. From our view, the only place for the corporation is in business planning – and even then the corporation is less frequently the entity of choice for most small businesses.

When is a business too small to incorporate?

No business is too small to incorporate because no business is safe from lawsuits. Obviously, the larger enterprise has more need for corporate protection if only because it is a larger lawsuit target, but still no business, no matter how small or seemingly safe, is immune from legal and financial disasters. Here is why we say *no* business is safe. A wealthy widow from our neighborhood, and a client, enjoyed spending her weekends selling imported dolls at a local flea market. Not long ago she sold a defective doll. A customer's three-year-old daughter punctured her eye after dislocating the doll's arm, exposing a large nail. This lady is now defending herself and her insignificant wealth against a $5 million products liability claim.

Had she incorporated her tiny kiosk enterprise, her corporation, and not herself, would have the liability; her personal assets would not be in jeopardy. Why *didn't* she incorporate? Her accountant discouraged her. "You don't need a corporation. Why spend money to incorporate to run a nickel-and-dime weekend business?" Bad advice! Had she incorporated, she would not be worried sick about losing everything she owns. Incorporating is your *best* insurance!

Is an S corporation as protective as a regular C corporation?

S and C corporations provide the same limited liability. They differ only in how they are taxed. There are also restrictions as to who can be stockholders in an S corporation. One restriction is that S corporation shares cannot be owned by other entities. That limits your ability to protect your stock ownership.

It sounds then that while you may recommend a corporation to conduct a business, would you normally use one to protect your personal assets?

No. For a corporation to give you inside protection, you must transfer your personal wealth to the corporation. You would then no longer personally own your boat, car, paintings, etc.; instead your corporation would. Your personal creditor could not directly claim the assets owned by the corporation, however, they could seize your corporate shares. That's the problem. Your ownership interest in the corporation can be seized and controlled by your personal creditor. If you own a controlling interest in the corporation, your creditor would indirectly control your corporation's assets. So you can never safely use the corporation alone to protect your personal assets. You must use a corporation in combination with other asset protection tools to adequately shield your personal assets. Nevertheless, a corporation can provide temporary shelter for personal assets. For instance, one memorable client transferred $100,000 to a Nevada corporation only two days before a creditor won a sizeable judgment against him. Had the client kept the bank account titled in his own name, the creditor would have immediately levied the account. But with his funds temporarily titled to a corporate account in another state, the creditor would first have to go through discovery before the creditor could find and seize the corporate shares. Of course, this gave us ample time to create a safer repository for his money.

In sum, the problem with using a corporation to protect personal assets is that you literally 'chase your tail.' While your assets are no longer exposed, your shares are instead vulnerable. For protection, you must then find ways to protectively title your corporate shares, as they cannot be owned by you personally.

What is a family limited partnership and what role does it play in asset protection?

A family limited partnership (FLP) is a limited partnership (LP) owned by family members, or family controlled entities (trusts, etc.). They work the same as any limited partnership. The FLP is commonly used for protection because it can protect a wide range of assets, maximize your creditor protection, minimize your estate taxes, and give you or your family continuing control over your assets.

For many years, the limited partnership has been a staple of asset protection planning. Although in many instances the limited liability company (LLC) is now

54

preferable to the LP, limited partnerships are still popular, and are sometimes still the entity of choice, especially for the reduction of estate taxes.

Limited partnerships are a variation of the general partnership. General partnerships (commonly referred to as 'partnerships') have existed for thousands of years. They are typically small businesses wherein each partner may manage, act for, and bind the company. Although a general partnership is technically not a distinct artificial entity, as it is not created by the government, each partner usually contributes property to a general pool of partnership assets as necessary for it to conduct business, and it is often treated as a distinct entity. General partnerships are often very basic and informal in their structure, and are thus easy to form and operate, requiring a minimum of associated paperwork aside from filing partnership tax returns.

As commercial law developed, general partnerships gradually began to demonstrate some glaring shortcomings. That brought about the limited partnership. Among these shortcomings is the fact that one partner can make a decision that could financially harm not only the partnership as a whole, but the personal wealth of the other partners. Like a sole proprietorship, general partnerships have no limited liability. Therefore, if one partner obligates the partnership to debts it cannot pay, the personal wealth of all partners is at risk of being forfeited to the partnership's creditors. The same is true with debts arising from lawsuits: if one partner is dishonest or commits a tort while working for the partnership, then a creditor could obtain a judgment against the wrongdoer, the partnership as a whole, as well as each individual partner.

The limited partnership's chief difference from the general partnership is that it has two classes of partners: General partners and limited partners. A general partner manages the company. However, the general partner has unlimited personal liability. Consequently, if the company is unable to pay its debts, its creditors can look only to the property of a general partner to satisfy those debts.

Limited partners do not have this same vulnerability. A creditor can only pursue a limited partner's assets to the extent those assets have been contributed to the partnership. This makes their liability similar to a corporate stockholder. This idea has been codified in the ULPA and its successors. At the same time, a limited partner is forbidden from managing or otherwise running the company. If a limited partner does manage the company then he will likely lose his limited liability.

Because general partners – even in a limited partnership – have unlimited liability, an LLC or corporation is often used as the general partner of an LP. This effectively gives the general partner limited liability. Although the LLC or corporation has unlimited liability for the debts of the LP, those debts do not generally extend to the owners or managers of the LLC or corporation. This arrangement is especially useful if multiple individuals manage the partnership. Instead of each person acting as a general partner where their actions could expose the other general partners to liability, they can each be a manager of a single LLC, a corporate officer, or board member of a single corporation. This would limit their exposure to the wrongful acts of the other managers, and allow everyone to participate in managing the LP.

Besides the distinction between limited and general partners, a limited partnership essentially operates like a general partnership. Consequently, LPs (before LLCs became popular) were often the entity of choice for small businesses. The reasons for this are threefold: Simple management structure, lack of a requirement to follow corporate formalities, and partnership tax (pass-through) treatment.

How does the FLP protect assets?

The short answer is that a limited partnership interest cannot be claimed by the debtor-partner's creditors. The creditor can only obtain a charging order which entitles the creditor only to whatever profit distributions are made to the debtor-partner. But this is usually an empty remedy since few FLPs make profit distributions when one partner has a charging order creditor and the FLP is managed by the debtor-partner or her family members.

Though we have discussed several benefits of the LP, we have not yet discussed its biggest benefit from an asset protection perspective. This benefit is the charging order. To say the charging order is a benefit is actually a bit of a misnomer, because in actuality the charging order is a remedy available to creditors. However, the remedy is so limited that it is often ineffective. That is why, amongst the over 20,000 entities we have created for clients (most of which were susceptible to a creditor's charging order), very few clients have been subject to a charging order. Furthermore, if the LP is created and operated correctly, a creditor has no other way to reach LP assets other than the charging order.

So what is the charging order? The charging order is a statutory provision of law under the UPA, ULPA, RULPA, and Revised Uniform Limited Liability Company Act (RULLCA) which provides a creditor of a company's partner or owner may attach company distributions made to that individual. However, this is generally the *only* remedy available to the creditor. This is so because it would be unfair to the other partners – or to the partnership itself – if a creditor were able to disrupt partnership business. This would harm the other partners who are not parties to the debt. Consequently, the charging order does *not* allow the creditor to control the entity, attach the entity's assets, or become a partner or owner of the entity. Of critical importance is the fact that, since a charging order holder cannot control the entity, they cannot control its profit distributions. In other words, if the entity never makes a distribution to the debtor-partner, then the creditor never receives a distribution. Their charging order then is essentially worthless. But a note of caution here: It is not a good idea to make distributions to all partners *except* the partner whose interest has been assigned to a creditor via a charging order. A judge might see this as an overt attempt to thwart the creditor from receiving his due. In such an instance, it is conceivable that a judge could view such circumstances as being akin to a fraudulent transfer which might then lead the court to force a distribution from the entity. If someone wishes to have distributions made to the other partners or owners while keeping his distribution out of the hands of his creditors, then before the creditor threat arises, the partner should place his partnership interest in another entity that is also protected by the charging order. The distributions will then be made to the second entity and not to the individual directly.

Can you give an example of how the FLP would be used in this instance?

Usually, spouses transfer most of their assets to the FLP. The spouses, as general partners, would share control. They may own their limited partnership interest personally or through their respective living trusts, or through other types of trusts. This arrangement provides excellent creditor protection, retained control, probate avoidance, and potential estate tax savings. Any other trust or entity can be limited partner(s). You can see that the FLP can be structured in many different ways.

Can one individual set up an FLP?

A partnership's definition requires 'two or more partners.' However, a corporation or LLC owned by the individual can become the general partner, and the individual personally, or through his living trust, may be the limited partner. We then have two owners. We have many similar organizational options.

Do other entities limit creditors to a charging order?

Because proper planning turns the charging order from a creditor remedy to a shield against creditors, any entity to which a charging order may apply is called a 'Charging Order Protected Entity' or COPE. COPES include; limited partnerships; limited liability partnerships; limited liability limited partnerships; or limited liability companies (in some jurisdictions, only multi-member LLCs have charging order protection).

Corporations are *not* COPES. As we have previously said, if a corporate shareholder comes under creditor attack, that creditor may seize his shares of stock for the amount of the outstanding debt. If the shares seized exceed 50 percent of the company's voting shares, the creditor could then vote to liquidate the company, and seize his share of the company assets upon liquidation. You can see why the vulnerability of corporate shares to creditor attachment makes the corporation a relatively poor protective vehicle for personal assets. This inability to seize COPE interests is what makes these entities so desirable for creditor protection.

How does a limited liability company differ from a limited partnership?

A limited liability company (LLC) is a hybrid between a corporation and limited partnership and it features the advantages of each. LLC managers have no personal liability for the debts of the LLC. This compares to officers and directors of a corporation. However, general partners of an LP are personally liable for the partnership debts. LLC membership interests have the same protection as do LP interests. The LLC member's creditor only has the same charging order remedy.

Why then use LPs instead of LLCs?

LLCs are becoming more popular and are fast replacing LPs. We almost always use LLCs to title non-residential real estate and to operate businesses but we still prefer LPs to title 'safe' liquid assets, particularly when their owners have a taxable estate. The LP has a long track record for protection and, in some states, provides superior protection over the LLC. But there are many tax, financial planning, regulatory and other considerations when choosing an entity. So a comprehensive plan for a client may include a number of different entities – S and C corporations, LPs, LLCs, trusts, and so forth.

Many practitioners prefer to use an FLP instead of an LLC for estate tax reduction. This is because FLPs are 'tried and true' and have a plethora of case law to support their efficacy. However, it is possible to structure an LLC like an FLP for the purposes of estate tax reduction. There is no case or statutory law that would prohibit this. At the same time, LLCs have not been as battle-proven in court as has the FLP.

To make certain an LLC is taxed like an FLP, it should be structured like an FLP. Namely, the company should have limited members (a 'member' is the LLC's equivalent to a partner) and managing members, and it should be taxed as a partnership. It should also have all the characteristics of an FLP.

With the more battle-tested track record of the FLP, one might ask: Why would anyone wish to form an LLC instead of an FLP? An LLC has some other benefits that an FLP does not. We can mention three: First, the LLC may exist perpetually (LPs typically may only exist for 30 years). Secondly, the LLC enjoys limited liability for managing members as well as limited members. Remember, the general partner (manager) of an LP has unlimited liability. Thirdly, after the death of the partner, an LLC may elect to be taxed as a C or S corporation. An LP must use partnership taxation without exception.

How do S corporations and LLCs differ?

An LLC is a similar entity to an S corporation since the owners of both entities enjoy limited liability and both entities can be taxed as either a proprietorship or partnership. An LLC member's risk is also limited to his loss of investment. However, a chief protective advantage of the LLC over the S corporation is that the LLC affords you more ownership options. For example, your LLC can be owned by a family limited partnership (FLP), a trust, another corporation, etc. S corporation shares cannot be owned by these entities. Their stock ownership is restricted to individuals. Both estate and asset protection planning then become more difficult with S corporation shares.

More importantly, an ownership interest in an LLC is considerably more creditor protected than are shares in an S corporation which can be easily seized by a stockholder's personal creditors. A member's interest in an LLC is creditor protected in the same way a partnership interest in a limited partnership is protected. A member's personal creditor is limited only to a charging order against the LLC interest, which gives the creditor only the right to receive distributed profits due the debtor partners.

There are still a few advantages of an S corporation over an LLC: (1) An S corporation can be more tax advantageously acquired by another business; (2) S corporation owners pay employment taxes only on *their* salaries, while LLC owners pay employment taxes on *all* profits; and (3) State taxes may be lower for an S corporation.

It seems there are subtle differences between FLPs, LLCs, corporations and the other entities we often hear about. How can we decide which is best for us in a given situation?

It can be difficult to decide upon the right entity in a given situation. You will probably need both your attorney and accountant to sort through their relative advantages and disadvantages of each entity as it applies to your situation. Or go online to www.AssetProtectionAttorneys.com for a fuller explanation of each of these entities.

But as we stated, it is not unusual for clients with more complex holdings to use all these and other entities. For example, we may set up a limited partnership to own a client's 'safe' assets (investments, etc.) and the client's ownership interests in LLCs or C corporations. We may have a number of LLCs (one for each business or real estate investment) or C corporation interests. An S corporation may fit into the equation for tax reasons. The limited partnership interest, in turn, may be owned by a living trust or a domestic or international asset protection trust for added protection or probate avoidance. The planning possibilities using these different entities are endless. So the decision of choice of entity should not be exclusively a legal decision. Since the decision also involves taxes, operational, regulatory and other factors it then necessitates involving the client's accountant, business lawyer, and possibly the client's estate and/or financial planner as well.

What is the role of domestic trusts in asset protection planning?

They play a relatively minor role. There are hundreds of different trusts, and each has its specific purpose for estate or financial planning. But for creditor protection, the trust must be *irrevocable* and *intervivos* – or funded during your lifetime. Until you transfer your assets to the trust, your assets, of course, are subject to the claims of your personal creditors.

There are other limitations to the use of trusts to shield one's assets. The trust cannot ordinarily be settled for the sole benefit of the grantor. A grantor seeking lawsuit protection can retain no beneficial interest – though some retention of income rights based on some ascertainable standard (health needs, etc.) may still allow the trust to provide protection. Most states disallow self-settled trusts for asset protection. The grantor cannot control the trust nor have any beneficial rights.

Moreover, assets transferred to an irrevocable trust may be subject to fraudulent transfer claims by the grantor's creditors. Present creditors –known or unknown – can recover fraudulent transfers. That's why you must transfer assets to a domestic irrevocable trust only when you're certain you have no *present* creditors. But how can you ever know this beforehand? For these reasons, unless the trust provides other estate planning or tax benefits, we wouldn't normally use a domestic *irrevocable intervivos* trust solely to protect a client's assets. The LP or LLC is preferable. However, revocable trusts can shield your children's inheritance and protect your estate. And special purpose trusts, such as irrevocable life insurance trusts, might own your life insurance. For these reasons we generally don't use irrevocable trusts to protect our clients' assets from *their* creditors but do recommend trusts to protect significant trust assets from their beneficiaries' lawsuits, creditors, and ex-spouses. These beneficiaries are usually the grantor's children or grandchildren.

This doesn't diminish the role of domestic trusts in our planning. We do use scores of different trusts and each has its application – whether for estate, tax or philanthropic purposes. And some of these trusts do provide protection. But when we use these trusts it is ordinarily for some purpose other than the protection of the settlor's assets. Protection becomes a secondary or incidental benefit.

When you do think about trusts for protection, you must consider them from several perspectives: 1) Which trusts can protect the assets from the grantor's creditors? 2) Which trusts can protect the assets from the beneficiaries' creditors? 3)

How can you improve the protection afforded by a particular trust? 4) What protection can you expect from the more commonly used trust? We will, of course, talk more about trusts, particularly when we talk about how to protect your estate and inheritance.

You mention 'going international' with your money. Can you give us an overview?

Our many years as asset protection and wealth preservation lawyers have taught us that the safest wealth is *international* wealth. We create international asset protection programs for many clients and none has lost their international assets to *any* litigant. These clients also enjoy greater privacy and more than a few find investing internationally to be more profitable.

Your money is far safer internationally than it is in lawsuit-crazed America. Yes, you must pay your taxes on your international income and follow a few tax reporting rules, but it's all 100 percent legitimate. If your accountant or lawyer thinks international finance is only for crooks, frauds, and the super-rich, they would be wrong, and their narrow mindedness could cost you your wealth.

International wealth protection is increasingly popular and will continue to grow in importance and popularity because financial and legal professionals want stronger protection for their clients. Unfortunately, too many lawyers still rely entirely on domestic asset protection strategies when their clients' money would be considerably safer internationally. That's why when we protect our wealthier clients we frequently blend domestic and international strategies. We use the domestic strategies to shelter their U.S.-based assets, such as real estate and their business, and their international entities protect their nest egg and liquid investments. This combination creates the most effective overall protection.

What type client uses international financial planning?

Not surprisingly, most of America's major corporations have international entities. And no less conspicuous are the hundreds of thousands of ordinary people worried about litigation and loss of their wealth. They want the *best* protection – and they find it internationally. For instance, one advantage of international protection is that fraudulently transferred assets within the U.S. are recoverable through the U.S. courts which have jurisdiction over these assets. But American courts lack jurisdiction over international assets, which makes them far better protected. This point is important. You never know when someone will raise claims from the past.

International Financial Centers provide powerful debtor protection because they impose many legal and procedural obstacles which few creditors can overcome. One example is their short statute of limitations (one or two years) to challenge asset transfers internationally. Timely challenges are rare. Another obstacle is that creditors must *prove beyond a reasonable doubt* that a transfer internationally was fraudulent which is a very difficult standard to overcome. Nevis is a particularly strong asset protection jurisdiction and it makes the creditor post a cash bond before the creditor can sue. Another roadblock is that a creditor must hire local counsel on a fee-only basis as contingent fees aren't allowed. Moreover, a judgment creditor must sue anew in the international jurisdiction as these asset protection centers do not recognize or enforce US judgments. We can continue and cite many other reasons why international protection is so formidable.

In sum, people who go internationally with their money are those with enough wealth to make it worthwhile, say $500,000 or more. These people rightfully want appreciably stronger protection than domestic or U.S.-based entities can provide.

As we later discuss in the chapter on *Protecting Your Investments* you will see how international planning works in greater detail. Our website www.AssetProtectionAttorneys.com also fully discusses the various international entities. The point is that international wealth protection can be both vital and complex, but deserves investigation and consideration if you have sufficient liquid

64

assets that need the strongest possible protection.

Finally, you mention equity stripping as a method to shield assets. How does this work?

This strategy calls for you to borrow against or otherwise pledge your assets as collateral security for some obligation. The secured creditor then has first claim against the asset to the extent of the loan. If the loan approximates the value of the asset, there is little or no equity exposed to a litigant. These loans can be structured in a number of ways. It's possible to fully encumber everything you own through one or more loans, and this is a common defensive technique when you anticipate serious problems.

Too many attorneys overlook the equity stripping strategy when they attempt to shelter their clients' assets. But equity stripping combined with titling assets to protective entities can be just the combination needed to stop even the most determined creditor. Part of the problem is that lawyers may see equity stripping as a financial – not legal – solution. A more common problem is that few attorneys – or clients – know how to structure liens that are both defensible and workable from the client's perspective. But we will talk more about this too throughout the interview and the reader will see how they can equity strip every asset they own and thereby create an insurmountable obstacle to any creditor.

I appreciate that this is only a broad overview of the more common planning tools, but are there others?

We have covered only some of the available options. We call them the foundational tools. But any expert in our field can go far beyond these basics. And it is no different with us. There are scores of other legal devices. And more and more frequently our strategies are financial in nature. That's why our firm includes sophisticated financial planners who can often bring to the client's situation some tremendously creative solutions. As the expression goes "there are many ways to skin a cat". Our job is to do it in a way that will give our clients the best protection legally possible.

4

Protecting

The Family Home

Now that you explained some basic and general ways to shelter your assets, let's talk about the more common methods to protect specific assets, starting with the family home.

First, how vulnerable is the family home to lawsuits?

Most Americans consider their home to be their most valuable – and vulnerable asset. Certainly, it's the one asset of greatest concern when they are sued because they are most emotionally attached to their home. The home is also vulnerable to lawsuits because it's usually titled personally to their owners since personal ownership may be necessary for conventional home financing and to claim the federal capital gains tax benefits, homestead protection, and real estate tax abatements available to seniors. Finally, the home is vulnerable because it can be readily attached simply by filing a judgment with the county recorder. This effectively transfers the home's equity to the creditor.

How do people typically lawsuit-proof their home?

It's not that difficult to minimize the home equity that is exposed to creditors. One can accomplish it in a number of ways. But combining mortgages against the home with the protection of their state's homestead laws are the two chief strategies. This dual strategy would leave little or no equity exposed. However, one can take a number of other steps to protect their home with exposed equity.

How protective are the homestead laws?

The state homestead laws may partly or fully creditor protect the home's equity. Five states *totally* homestead protect the home; however, most state homestead laws only partly creditor shield the home. The state homestead laws vary greatly in how much home equity they protect. Homestead laws, in all instances, apply only to the home or primary residence. You must own *and* occupy the property as your home. Other restrictions may limit your homestead protection. For example, Florida protects an unlimited home equity; however, the acreage must fall under certain limits. Lot size is a common restriction. If your home qualifies for *some* homestead protection, you must determine how much equity it protects. Most states lawsuit-proof between $5,000 and $50,000 in equity. So for homes with a large equity, the homestead laws may be nearly worthless. However, if you live in Texas, Florida or other states that fully homestead protects the home, you have an exceptionally strong firewall. A number of states generously homestead up to $500,000 or more in equity.

The homestead laws can raise more questions than they answer. For instance, Florida recently ruled that one property used for a home, commercial farm and guest house qualified the entire property for homestead. But is a houseboat homestead protected? To answer these questions you have to thoroughly check your state statutes and case law.

Would bankruptcy alter my homestead protection?

Recent federal bankruptcy amendments limit the state homestead exemption to $146,450 if you purchased your residence within the 40 months preceding bankruptcy. You must also have lived in that state for 730 days. This new bankruptcy amendment prevents debtors from last minute 'forum shopping' to evade creditors, by using their exposed assets to buy expensive homes immediately before filing bankruptcy. Still, many people continue to move to Florida to buy expensive homes that are fully protected. The new bankruptcy law leaves several issues unsettled. If you sell one homestead home and use the proceeds to buy another home, does the 40 months start anew? Can you safely use your exposed cash to reduce your home mortgage within the 40 months? Can you safely use the cash to improve your home? These and similar issues concerning the scope of homestead protection await court rulings at both the state and federal levels.

If a home has a homestead exemption of more than $146,450; won't this exemption still apply if you don't file bankruptcy within 40 months?

Yes. However, a judgment creditor can often force a debtor into involuntary bankruptcy within the 40 months to limit the homestead exemption to $146,450. This would then expose any additional equity. That's why you must take other steps to shelter the exposed equity from this contingency and cannot always rely on homestead protection.

How do I calculate my exposed home equity?

Simply subtract your mortgage from your home's fair market value. A $300,000 home with a $150,000 mortgage has a $150,000 equity. If your state homestead law shelters $20,000, you have a $130,000 equity vulnerable to a lawsuit.

What procedural steps are necessary to claim homestead protection?

Most states impose procedural requirements for one to claim homestead protection. Usually, you must file a declaration of homestead in the public registry. Other states impose a residency period before they grant homestead protection. You can never assume that your home is automatically protected. You must check your state's specific requirements.

Can married couples apply their homestead exemption against the debts of only one spouse?

State laws do differ on who can claim the homestead protection. Several states give homestead protection only to the head of the household, but most states allow either spouse to claim homestead. This is certainly the trend. Several states cancel homestead protection when it is separately applied for by both spouses, as cross-declarations cancel each other. Other states allow co-owner spouses to apportion their homestead protection against their respective ownership interests. In these instances, the spouse should consider which spouse should claim the homestead exemption. If your state allows spousal apportionment, the homestead protection should logically be allocated to the greater lawsuit risk spouse.

Are there ways to maximize your homestead protection?

There are several interesting techniques to maximize your homestead protection. For example, if your $200,000 home has $50,000 homestead protection and a $100,000 mortgage, you have $50,000 equity exposed to creditors. One way to shelter this $50,000 equity is to increase your mortgage from $100,000 to $150,000 and invest the $50,000 loan proceeds in other exempt assets, or you can protect the cash proceeds using the protective strategies we suggest to protect cash and liquid investments. Or if you have a substantial or unlimited homestead protection – as in Texas and Florida – a good strategy may be to refinance or sell your non-exempt assets, such as a vacation home, car or boat, and buy a home. Or you may improve your home or reduce your mortgage since your home is fully homestead protected regardless of value.

Does the homestead exemption protect against every creditor?

No. Some creditors can override homestead protection and claim your home equity. These creditors include the IRS and other federal agencies. If you owe federal taxes or are sued by the SEC or the EPA, for example, you might lose your home. Also, your homestead laws may or may not protect your home from the state tax collector. This depends on your state law. Spouses in a divorce or family members who challenge their inheritances can also override the homestead laws, as can plaintiffs suing for intentional torts (libel, fraud, deceit, etc.). Of course, mortgages or deeds of trust, voluntarily granted to creditors as collateral, are unaffected by homestead. These lenders have full recourse to the home as do creditors where you specifically waive your homestead protection. Some state homestead laws also only protect the home against debts incurred *after* the homestead protection was claimed. This is a common restriction.

If my home equity is now fully homestead protected, do I need more protection?

You may. Homestead protection can be illusory. For example, if you have a $300,000 home equity and a $300,000 homestead exemption, your home is *now* fully protected. But how well will your home be protected in the future? You'll build equity in your home each month through its appreciating value and by reducing its mortgage. If you are sued years from now, you'll have substantially more equity which your homestead exemption won't cover. Homesteading seldom fully protects the family home, so one solution is to periodically refinance your home so that your combined mortgages *and* your state homestead exemption together leave no equity exposed to a lawsuit. You also need other means of protection when your creditor is unaffected by homestead.

If I sell my home, how do I shelter the proceeds?

When you sell or refinance your homesteaded home, you should shelter the proceeds. You have options: One option is to use the proceeds from the sale or refinancing to buy another exempt asset. For example, you might use the protected proceeds from selling your homesteaded home to buy an exempt annuity. Or you might invest the proceeds in a protective entity, such as a limited partnership, LLC or irrevocable trust. Most homestead law states protect the proceeds from the sale or refinancing of an exempt asset either for a specified time (set by statute) or for a reasonable time (determined by the courts). But for continued protection of the proceeds, you must segregate the exempt proceeds in separate accounts so it can be identified as proceeds from an exempt asset.

Is it a good idea to title the family home to the spouse with less lawsuit exposure?

Commonly the family residence is titled to the less liability prone spouse. While this makes the home safer, it has drawbacks. One drawback is that you can't be certain that this spouse will remain liability free. You also run the risk that if you divorce, your spouse may sell or refinance the home and dissipate the proceeds. To prevent this, you may encumber the home to an entity that you control. Another disadvantage is that when marital assets are titled to only one spouse it frustrates good estate planning. By equally dividing marital assets, you can more tax-efficiently plan your estate. Finally, creditors of the non-title spouse may argue that the funds used to buy or maintain the home came from the debtor-spouse, and therefore, that spouse – and his creditors – has an equitable interest in the home. For these reasons, titling the home and other marital assets to the less vulnerable spouse is not always sound planning.

My state allows spouses to title their homes as tenants-by-the-entirety. How good is this protection?

Tenancy-by-the-entirety is a special type of joint tenancy reserved for husbands and wives – recognized in twenty-five eastern states. Some tenants-by-the-entirety laws provide no more creditor protection than will joint tenancy – that is, little or none. However, property titled to both spouses as tenancy-by-the-entirety in other states enjoys relatively strong lawsuit protection. Generally, a creditor of only *one* spouse cannot claim that debtor-spouse's interest in the tenancy-by-the-entirety property. But a creditor of *both* spouses can claim tenancy-by-the-entirety property. For example, if the husband and wife both guaranteed a bank note, the bank could claim the couple's tenancy-by-the-entirety property. If only one spouse guaranteed the note, then titling the asset as tenancy-by-the-entirety would lawsuit-protect it against that creditor.

If your state's tenancy-by-the-entirety laws can protect you, then re-title the jointly-owned home to yourself and your spouse as tenancy-by-the-entirety. But have your attorney decide whether a tenancy-by-the-entirety titled home in your state will adequately shield it. Also, bear in mind that when one spouse dies, the tenancy-by-the-entirety titled home will automatically pass to the surviving spouse and then become vulnerable to the surviving spouse's creditors. Nor can you bequeath tenancy-by-the-entirety assets to other beneficiaries. If this isn't your wish, then don't title the home – or any other asset – as tenancy-by-the-entirety.

Spouses in states with strong tenancy-by-the-entirety laws frequently rely on it to lawsuit protect their home and other assets. However, we have seen some erosion in tenants-by-the-entirety protection. Several bankruptcy courts have ruled that a bankruptcy trustee can, in some circumstances, claim the tenants-by-the-entirety interest owned by the bankrupt spouse. The IRS can also seize a tenants-by-the-entirety interest owned by a delinquent taxpayer, even if the spouse owes no taxes.

If your state's tenancy-by-the-entirety laws protects the home, the couple should only title their home or any other asset as tenancy-by-the-entirety when: 1) the couple intends survivorship rights to the asset; 2) the spouses have low liability exposure, and aren't likely to incur significant joint obligations; and 3) the couple is reasonably young and are less concerned that one spouse may unexpectedly die and leave the property exposed to the surviving spouse's judgment creditors.

When should someone title their home to a protective entity, such as a limited partnership or limited liability company?

Both the limited liability company and limited partnership similarly protect assets, however we wouldn't normally title a client's home to a family limited partnership or multi-member limited liability company for their charging order protection. Asset protection planners occasionally do recommend titling the family residence to a limited partnership, but the downside is that you lose your homeowner tax benefits. However, you can maintain your home ownership tax benefits if you title your home to a *single-member* limited liability company which is considered a disregarded entity for tax purposes. These tax benefits can be considerable.

For example, a single person has $250,000 capital gains tax exclusion on the profits when they sell their home. A married couple has a $500,000 exclusion. To claim this exclusion: 1) one or both spouses must have owned the home for at least two out of the five years preceding the sale; and 2) the house must be the primary residence during those years. If a family limited partnership owns the house for more than three of those five years, the owners lose their tax benefit. They can, however, transfer their home to a family limited partnership for no more than three years and then retransfer the home back to their name for at least two years; however, this arrangement is usually impractical and burdensome.

It's sometimes smart to have a single-member limited liability company own the home. If you're married, one spouse (usually the less liability-prone spouse) can be that single-member, though this is not always the preferred strategy. The IRS disregards single-member limited liability companies for tax purposes, so the home, for capital gains purposes, should be considered as if the home were owned by the individual member. You cannot achieve this tax strategy with a limited partnership which requires at least two owners and therefore cannot be a disregarded entity. We urge our readers to review this strategy carefully with their tax advisor. But remember: If you title your home to a single-member LLC, you may lose your homestead protection.

The single-member LLC is protective to the extent that it will shield the home from adverse judgments filed against the debtor as the prior owner. On the other hand, courts have sometimes set aside singe-member LLCs, and the single-member may then possibly be successfully creditor challenged.

Are there ways to build on the protection of the single-member LLC?

There are a number of ways to strengthen the arrangement. One way is to have the LLC that owns the home fully-owned by an international asset protection trust. Some advisors title the home directly to the international trust, but this can prove unwieldy since an international trustee firm must then administer the property. In all instances, a creditor can recover the home if it was fraudulently transferred to the LLC, an international trust or any other entity or party. That's why we also equity

73

strip the home. There's no equity in the home to seize even if the property is recovered.

Wouldn't encumbering my home be a good way to protect it? If so wouldn't it make sense to get a line of credit secured by the home?

It makes a lot of sense for the reasons we just explained. We advise our clients to *always* keep their home fully encumbered by mortgages even if they must periodically refinance their mortgages to cover their equity as their home value increases. You may ask: "Why pay interest on a loan that I don't need to protect myself against a lawsuit that may never happen?" Great question! Refinancing your home to reduce your exposed equity may not make *financial* sense even when it makes *legal* sense, but a *home equity* line of credit is always sensible when you're not fully homestead protected. For instance, a $200,000 mortgage free home should qualify for a $150,000 home equity loan or line of credit. You owe your lender nothing and pay no interest until you actually borrow against your credit line, which you would do only if you're sued. A prospective litigant checking your assets would see that you have only a $50,000 equity in your home because of the recorded $150,000 mortgage. You are then a less attractive lawsuit candidate. An equity loan, line of credit or reverse mortgage can cover much of your home equity. Once the loan is in place, you can quickly draw down the line of credit if you are sued and can protect the cash proceeds as you would your other liquid assets.

What if a home equity line of credit covers only part of the equity? How do you shelter the remaining equity?

Your goal is to have your home 100 percent encumbered. Shopping for a second or third mortgage is one possibility. Lenders may loan up to 90-95 percent of value if you have good credit. Or you can pledge other assets to further collateralize the home loan. A co-signer might get you a 100 percent loan. Executory obligations can also be consideration to support a mortgage. There are hundreds of ways to fully encumber a home – or any other asset.

In practice, a home mortgaged to about 85 percent of value should be adequately collateralized. Homes seldom yield more at auction. Your homestead protection may also cover the remaining equity in your home, and if so you would need a far lower loan to shield the exposed equity. You can equity-strip or encumber your home even after you are sued and this wouldn't be a fraudulent transfer since you received simultaneous consideration for the mortgage – the loan.

But how feasible is it to get a 90-100 percent loan? What if you have poor credit, low income or the inability to pay the loan?
That's another excellent and common question. You may not be a good candidate for conventional financing, but there are a host of unconventional financing arrangements that can be used to create valid, protective liens. The point is that a knowledgeable asset protection planner will know how to equity-strip the home – or any other asset – notwithstanding a client's credit standing, income or ability to repay the loan.

The important point is that a mortgages against your home – or any other asset – must be fully supported by consideration. You must give something of equivalent value for the loan. You can't simply have someone file a mortgage or deed of trust against your home and expect it to work. Creditors can and do challenge sham or phony mortgages.

I have read that some people title their home to personal residence trusts to save estate taxes and also for protection. How do these trusts work?
Older people sometimes want to protect their home and lower their estate taxes. A Qualified Personal Residence Trust (QPRT) may be their answer. Here, you transfer your residence to the trust and retain a tenancy for ten years. At the end of the ten years, the title to your residence passes to your beneficiaries. Your objective is to transfer your residence at its lower present value (basis), rather than when you die and your home has a greater taxable value. The QPRT thus freezes its value and reduces your estate taxes if you have a taxable estate. A QPRT can also lawsuit-protect

75

your home because your creditors can only claim your right to *use* the property for the remaining term of years (or the rental value for those years). However, your creditor cannot seize the home itself because it would be owned by the trust. Nor can the beneficial remainder interest be claimed by your beneficiaries' creditors if your trust includes spendthrift provisions. At the end of the term, the trustee must distribute the assets (the residence or cash proceeds from its sale) or convert the QPRT assets into an annuity which may be the more desirable alternative, if your state creditor protects annuities. However, if you die within the ten years, the trust ends and title to the property reverts to you.

Why couldn't I instead gift my home now and retain a life estate?

That strategy is similar to the qualified personal residence trust. You could gift your home – usually to your children – and retain a life estate. Though the life estate can be claimed by your creditors, you can avoid its seizure by pledging your life estate interest as collateral for a loan. Or you can lease-back the property for the term of your life through a protective entity – such as an LLC. You achieve a similar result by titling your home to an irrevocable trust and retaining a life estate. Your home would transfer to the trust beneficiaries upon your death. Still another variation on the theme is to sell your home to your children in exchange for a self-liquidating loan which can be cancelled during your lifetime or upon your death. Here, too, you would retain a life estate to the home.

Is my home protected if I title it to my living trust?

Because a living trust is usually a revocable trust, it will not provide protection. If you can revoke your trust, so can your creditors. Titling the home to a living trust can nevertheless be advantageous because the home will then avoid probate.

If I have several judgments against me and want to buy a home, how can I accomplish this without jeopardizing the home?

When you have severe creditor problems, your smartest option may be not to own your home. Lease a home with an option to buy. Have the option granted to an entity that you do not directly own. Once you resolve your creditor problems, you can exercise the option. Or a third party might buy the property through an LLC or land trust/LLC combination and directly or indirectly assign the option to you. There are numerous variations on this theme, but in no event should the option to buy the home extend directly to you because you'd then lose the option's economic benefit to your creditor or bankruptcy trustee.

Are there other ways to lawsuit-proof the family home?

Positively. Some planners, for example, title the home to international asset protection trusts – a strategy we generally do not use because it is cumbersome. Other planners use domestic asset protection trusts with the drawback that the trust is irrevocable.

We have hundreds of creative ways to keep the family home from the wolves. Sometimes the answer is common sense, such as leasing the home to a friend or relative for a low rent that would create a negative cash flow to the creditor who forecloses on his judgment.

I imagine many of your clients are 'upside-down' on their mortgages. What advice do you have for these clients?

You're right. Our clients now include many distressed property owners victimized by the real estate downturn. Of course, the first thing we do is to see if we can arrange a short sale or deed-in-lieu of foreclosure with the lender to eliminate the possibility of a deficiency. If a deficiency judgment appears likely, then we shelter any properties or any other assets the client owns that has a positive equity. Frequently, once the lender realizes that the borrower is judgment-proof, it is sufficient for the lender to accept the property and forego any recourse against the borrower on the deficiency. Readers who have mortgage problems can call our firm 561-953-1050.

In sum, it would seem that most homes can be protected through mortgages and state homestead laws which together reduce their equity to the point where the home is valueless to creditors. Is that correct?

As a general proposition, that's how we protect most of our clients' homes. Titling the property between spouses as tenants-by-the-entirety can also help as can creating an LLC to hold title – if a recorded lien, judgment or attachment would otherwise cloud title to the home.

5

Protecting
Non-Residential
Real Estate

How would one protect their vacation homes, rental properties or other commercial properties? Would we use the same strategies to protect these properties as we would our home?

The strategies we would use to protect your vacation home and investment real estate would follow different strategies than what we would use to lawsuit-proof your home. We use different strategies for the home because we want to preserve the home's tax benefits. That's why we would title the residence to your personal name or a single-member LLC. You also want to preserve your homestead protection. However, homestead protection and the homeowner's tax benefits don't extend to other real property. So we have different protective options for non-primary residence real estate. Investment properties, of course, can also impose more potential liabilities than will your residence, so you also want to personally protect yourself against the potential liabilities that arise from owning rental properties. Landlords have many potential liabilities. They get sued by tenants, tenants' guests, sub-lessees, neighbors, neighborhood associations, contractors and even trespassers. They are also sued for all sorts of property defects. And a landlord can be held 'strictly liable' whether or not the landlord acted negligently.

Protecting investment real estate is now a more important aspect of our practice because so many more individuals and families now own rental properties. It's often a significant portion of their net worth. This was less true in past generations when relatively few people owned income properties and second homes. 'Landlording' was then not so popular a business. But the surge in second residences, vacation homes, land speculation, property 'flipping,' development and other real estate pursuits brings to the forefront the need to protect – and be protected – from these properties. Fortunately, we have a number of good ways to accomplish this. Our present challenge is chiefly to protect the client's other wealth from their distressed property and the deficiencies on bank notes. These are interesting financial times – particularly for real estate investors.

What's the first step to protect these properties?

The first rule is to title all real estate that you own or co-own – other than your personal residence – to one or more limited liability companies (LLCs). This includes rental and commercial properties, land, vacation homes and time shares. Why is the LLC the ideal entity to own your investment real estate? Because it protects the owner(s) personally from liabilities originating from the property (as would a corporation), and, as importantly, it shelters the property and your interest in the LLC against claims by your personal creditors. The LLC, as with the limited partnership, is a charging order protected entity (COPE). COPE entities limit the creditor of an LLC member to a 'charging order'. The creditor can only claim profit distributions made from the LLC (or limited partnership) to that debtor-member. This is the creditor's sole remedy. The member's personal creditor cannot claim the LLC membership interest. However, the creditor can claim the stock ownership in a corporation. This is the major reason why we use the LLC to own non-residential property.

There are several other reasons we prefer an LLC over either a corporation or limited partnership as the entity for investment properties. You avoid double taxation with a limited liability company. Since the limited liability company isn't usually taxed as a corporation, you avoid the corporate income tax. Limited liability company income is usually taxed personally to its members. You also avoid personal liability with a limited liability company. LLC managers and members are personally protected from the LLC's creditors, even when the LLC members manage the company. Conversely, general partners of a limited partnership *are* personally liable for partnership debts. Limited partners of a limited partnership cannot manage the limited partnership without incurring personal liability, though you can avoid this personal exposure by forming a corporation or LLC to be the general partner.

As we mentioned earlier, the charging order is not usually an effective creditor remedy. It won't give the creditor voting rights. The LLC manager can't be forced to pay profit distributions to the members (or to the member's creditors). The LLC's charging order is usually as futile a creditor remedy as with limited partnerships. If you manage your LLC, you decide upon distributions. Your judgment creditor cannot vote you out as the manager because a member's creditor has no vote. For as long as your creditor has a charging order, you can withhold distributions. Nevertheless, you can compensate yourself (and other members) and pay yourself salaries for services, and use other indirect mechanisms to withdraw money from the LLC. Salaries cannot be claimed through the charging order, nor can loans or other compensation be paid to managers or members.

Clearly, for the family-owned income property, the LLC is the entity of choice. Few asset protection attorneys disagree. Larger real estate projects or entities with publicly-traded securities and outside investors may choose limited partnerships or real estate investment trusts (REITs). But the ownership interests in these entities can be similarly protected from creditor claim. If a debtor-member of a limited partnership or REIT cannot prevent profit distributions (which can be claimed by their creditors); they should have an LLC own their partnership interest or beneficial interest in the REIT so profit distributions flow to the LLC, not to the debtor-partner/beneficiary's creditor.

Should we title separate properties to separate LLCs?

Always segregate your properties by titling them to separate LLCs. For example, we would title 15 rental properties to 15 separate LLCs. The liability from any one property won't then jeopardize any other properties. Of course, you must then form and administer 15 LLCs. But to simplify matters, Delaware, Oklahoma and several other states allow you to set up what is called a 'Series LLC.' A Series LLC allows you to establish a series of 'cells' within each LLC. Each cell within the series operates as a distinct LLC. Each cell can own different properties or businesses, have different managers and members, and separate operating agreements with different provisions. They may file consolidated or separate tax returns and otherwise operate autonomously from the other cells within the series. Liabilities from the property in each cell thus remains confined to the assets within that one cell. Properties titled to the other cells remain safe from creditors from any other cell. Those who need multiple LLCs or own multiple properties should consider the Series LLC.

The Series LLC is a new entity. So, one problem is that it hasn't been fully court-tested concerning their liability protection from the creditors from 'different' cells within the series. Nevertheless, more states are considering Series LLC legislation. The Series LLC may be the entity of the future for real estate investors that own a number of properties. You can own hundreds of different properties within the same Series LLC. And forming a new cell within the Series is as easy as computer downloading the name of a new cell. Moreover, you can use a Series LLC to own property in any state. If your properties are located in different states, you'd register the LLC as an international LLC in each state where you own properties; however, you needn't register each cell in that state. The Series LLC thus lets you avoid the expense of forming multiple LLCs; however, for protection, you must operate each cell autonomously.

To what extent do you use Series LLCs in your practice to title separate properties?

Only to a minor extent and usually only when the client has a large number of low equity properties. We still suggest separate LLCs rather than a Series LLC because the Series LLC has not been fully tested as to whether the courts will isolate liabilities between cells. The bigger practical problem is that most lawyers, banks and title companies are unfamiliar with the Series LLC. This adds to the complexity of completing real estate transactions. Still, given time, we believe the Series LLC will grow in popularity.

How can I protect my membership interests in LLCs that own my real estate?

You would use most of the same strategies you'd use to increase your lawsuit protection as a shareholder of a corporation or limited partner in a limited partnership. For example, you can assess your membership interest; give voting proxies to third parties; grant options to the LLC to redeem your membership interest; encumber or lien your membership interest; or dilute your membership control by selling additional ownership interests. You can also more protectively title your membership interest. For instance, LLC membership interests owned by spouses can be titled as tenants-by-the-entirety in states that protect this form of marital ownership from lawsuits against one spouse. An international trust can also own your LLC membership interest in the same way an international trust can be the limited partner of your limited partnership (LP). Or a limited partnership can be the member of your LLC. We particularly recommend this in those states that better protect LP interests than LLC memberships. Frequently, living trusts are members of an LLC. This doesn't add lawsuit protection because a living trust isn't a protective entity, but the living trust allows the membership interest to pass to the trust's beneficiaries without probate upon the member's death. Irrevocable domestic asset protection trusts (DAPTs) provide greater protection, but their disadvantage is that they're not revocable.

For maximum protection, your LLC should have at least one member aside from the lawsuit defendant member. Courts are reluctant to expand upon a creditor's charging order remedy when non-debtor members would be affected. Conversely, courts are more likely to liquidate a single-member LLC, or allow foreclosure or surrender of the LLC interest, when the debtor is the sole member. You also need a well-drafted LLC operating agreement. Don't use an LLC 'off-the-shelf' operating agreement. You want an absolutely lawsuit-proof operating agreement for your LLC for optimum protection. Few standard operating agreements include these more protective provisions. And this is an important point. The protection afforded an LLC membership interest or limited partnership interest depends on whether the operating or limited partnership agreement contains these protective provisions. Yet they can mean the difference between keeping or losing your ownership interest to the entity. You definitely need a good asset protection attorney to prepare and to periodically review these agreements.

Do you ever title investment properties to limited partnerships?

Not generally. Before limited liability company laws were enacted, the limited partnership was the entity of choice to own investment properties because the only alternative was the corporation. However, the limited partnership offered the advantage of protecting the ownership interest in the entity since it was a COPE. Typically, a corporation was organized to be the general partner and hence, insulate those managing the general partner from partnership liabilities. But with the advent of the LLC over the last decade or two, the LLC has proven superior to own these properties because it is a COPE (which protects the members' ownership interest and the managers of the LLC have no personal liability).

But we do commonly have the membership interests in each LLC (holding a separate property) titled to one or more family limited partnerships. Consolidating the LLC ownership through one entity – the family limited partnership – accomplishes three things: 1) It simplifies administration and estate planning since only one entity (the limited partnership) owns all these individual entities; 2) the

84

partners of the limited partnership can get a reduced estate tax valuation because the LLC interests are pooled into the FLP which qualifies for the estate tax discount; and 3) we add another level of protection because a creditor must now pierce both the limited partnership and the LLC to reach the underlying properties. And in many states the protection for LPs are stronger than for LLCs.

Would titling my investment property to a land trust be preferable to an LLC?

Land trusts are chiefly used in Illinois, Florida, Georgia, California, Colorado and several other states, but can be used in any state. The land trust can own any type real estate, including the family home, but usually it's used only to title investment properties. A bank is normally the trustee. How well the land trust protects the beneficiaries' interest in real estate depends chiefly upon whether the trust contains spendthrift and anti-alienation provisions. As with any entity, the land trust must be properly drafted. As the trust beneficiary you wouldn't directly own the real estate. It would instead be titled to the trustee. You'd own only a beneficial interest in the trust. This is considered personal, not real property. But owning only a beneficial interest in a land trust doesn't, in itself, sufficiently protect you. Your personal creditors can usually seize this beneficial interest. You then need added protection. For this you would title your beneficial interest in the land trust to a limited partnership, LLC or irrevocable trust. You and your spouse can also own the beneficial interest as tenants-by-the-entirety if your state recognizes this form of ownership, and if it would sufficiently protect your interest.

As with LLCs, it's also best to use separate land trusts for each property. One limited partnership or LLC can be the beneficial owner for multiple trusts, though more cautious asset protection attorneys might suggest different LLCs (or different cells) within a Series LLC as the beneficiary of each land trust.

Land trusts are increasingly popular for real estate investors who want anonymity an extra layer of protection, since the property in trust wouldn't be directly connected to them through the public records. Privacy, not asset protection, is then the land trust's major advantage. The beneficial owners' names are not public record because the property is titled to the trustee. As secrecy aids asset protection, the land trust aids secrecy. However, there are two disadvantages with land trusts: First, they are costly to prepare and administer. Second, financing and managing the trust properties are also more cumbersome than properties titled to your own name, which is always a dangerous plan. We use land trusts to a limited extent.

Once we protectively title each property, should we reduce its exposed equity with debt-shields as you suggest with the family home?

Absolutely. You want to adopt the same equity reduction strategies you'd use with your home. The goal is to fully encumber your real estate. You want that profile of 'poverty' that discourages lawsuits. So that calls for third party liens against your investment properties. If you have good credit, you can borrow 70 percent or more of the properties' value from conventional lenders (banks, finance companies, etc.). With poor credit, or if you otherwise cannot obtain a conventional loan, 'hard money' lenders will lend at a steeper finance charge, which may still be preferable to losing your property in a lawsuit.

Though it's easy to understand the role of 'equity-stripping' in asset protection, the problem is implementation. You may not know how, or where, to find the right lenders. Or you may not know how to 'defensively position' and mortgage your property. But there are a number of different ways to structure secured real property loans. As with residential loans, we arrange loans and debt-shields for even the poorest credit risk property owners. Our financing arrangements involve third party guarantees, collateralizing the loan proceeds with 'back-to-back' loans, loans from international entities, and so forth. We also routinely encumber property through complex insurance/financing arrangements which fully encumber our clients' real estate. Debt-shielding commercial property, however, can be simpler. Start with banks, finance companies and conventional asset-based lenders. Or use an affiliated company as 'your lender' if you own smaller, less valuable properties.

86

We've debt-shielded the poorest credit risks from international lenders to legally and effectively encumber assets and estates worth millions. Our financing arrangements are generally tax-neutral, and neither saves nor defers taxes. For example, one car dealer in heavy litigation fully encumbered his $2 million home, vacation property, and car dealership valued over $6 million through a complex patchwork of cross-collateralized loans. Once his assets were fully encumbered, we settled a 20 million dollar lawsuit against him for only $100,000. Without these mortgages to shield his equity, the lawsuit would have cost him a fortune.

Equity-stripping is a vital strategy. We can arrange 95 percent loan/value mortgages against any type asset – real estate, a business, vehicles, notes receivable, intellectual property, and so forth. We can fully encumber and creditor proof virtually *every* U.S.-based asset. The loan proceeds are back-up collateral secured through an international trust. And a strong credit rating is unnecessary. Moreover, interest on the loan is set at about one-half percent, so your cash-flow impact within the loan term is minimal. This program is likely your best equity-stripping option if you have $500,000 or more in U.S.-based real estate or other assets that require protection.

Can a mortgage securing my real estate be based on consideration other than an actual loan?

Yes. 'Cash' loans most effectively equity-strip property, but they have their drawbacks. Your lender pays taxes on your interest payments, and you may not be able to fully encumber your assets through standard commercial lenders. You must also pay interest, or not have the credit, collateral or resources to fully equity-strip your property.

But obligations aside from cash loans can justify the lien. Liens secure a variety of obligations in the normal course of business. These executory obligations are as valid as cash loans. In fact, a lien securing an executory obligation is sometimes better than a lien securing a cash loan because there are generally no negative tax or economic consequences to fulfilling the obligation. You can also arrange for the lien not to be reduced until you fulfill your obligation. The lien amount can even grow until the obligation is fulfilled. You have no loan proceeds to protect, nor will cash shortages affect your ability to fulfill non-monetary obligations. You also need not worry about how to get $500,000 to equity-strip your $500,000 home or office building. Cash loans are easily quantified. You can't use a large lien to secure a small loan. However, executory obligations are difficult to quantify. You can easily match the obligation to the value of the encumbered property.

As with any strategy, there are alternate ways to achieve a specific objective or goal. Can your lien secure an existing loan? Can you give a lien to secure a contract, such as a lease, or subscription to buy an interest in another entity? What other obligations can you collateralize? What future or contingent liabilities might you secure?

We can arrange one loan package which would lien everything you own – your home, commercial properties, investments, vehicles, business interests and any other valuable asset. Titling each asset to its own best protective entity, and then creating an enforceable blanket lien is the ultimate asset protection plan – particularly when the equity in the form of the loan proceeds has been constructively shifted to an international asset protection entity.

Can I arrange loans against my properties by borrowing from relatives?
A debtor's family members – parents, siblings and other relatives – can encumber the debtor's property. Related parties are legally distinct parties. Liens or security interests between connected parties is enforceable provided there was adequate consideration for the loan. Of course, loans from family or affiliated parties will more likely be scrutinized by creditors as fraudulent transfers. 'Insider' loans are suspect – and should be. If a court finds that a loan is a sham and without fair consideration (an equivalent exchange of money, property or services), the mortgage will be nullified by the court. But even a spouse may encumber separately-owned property in 'common law' property states. Community property states allow only property that is owned and titled separately to be security for the other spouse.

One spouse can encumber assets of the other, but fraudulent transfer laws make these loans challengeable, particularly when the mortgage arose *after* the claim. An affiliated business that liens your property is also less easily defended if you own or control that business. Nevertheless, people do form corporations, limited partnerships and limited liability companies to hold a mortgage against their real estate. The mortgage may later be overturned by a court; still an asset search may not reveal the relationship between you and the lending entity. The lien thus provides protection to the extent it deters the less inquisitive plaintiff's lawyer seeking unencumbered assets. But it's faulty planning to rely on 'sham' mortgages that won't withstand judicial challenge.

If I put loans against my properties through affiliated lenders, isn't it safer to conceal my affiliation?

Yes, provided you don't commit perjury to maintain your secrecy. A more aggressive plan will reduce your visibility as the legal owner of the lending corporation, partnership or LLC. As a minority or invisible owner of the entity holding the mortgage, you wouldn't 'control' the corporation or LLC. Alternate arrangements are possible. For example, a decontrolled international corporation (an International Business Corporation, IBC) or LLC might encumber U.S. property. You want to structure the international entity to legally minimize the federal tax reporting requirements and the special anti-deferral tax rules that apply to international corporations, trusts and partnerships. You can also have several levels of customized international trusts, corporations, LLCs, private foundations or other entities to layer privacy and anonymity. However, don't use these techniques for tax avoidance. Get advice from a tax advisor familiar with the international reporting requirements.

International entities are frequently 'shell' IBCs or LLCs with neither shareholders nor capital. Only through intensive investigation can a creditor distinguish a shell entity from an operating entity. But even an international shell entity can provide reasonably good secrecy when used to encumber U.S. property. The success of this arrangement ultimately lies in the absolute privacy available from international financial centers, which deny plaintiffs' attorneys access to their records. A complex multiple layer international entity strategy completely severs relationships between your domestic LLC, as the U.S. property owner, and the international IBC or LLC holding liens against the property.

These equity reduction strategies sound complicated. How difficult are they to set up?

Structuring secured liens against investment property requires careful planning and attention to detail. You must also observe the applicable tax and other laws involved over the life of the lien. You must also clear a number of hurdles to avoid problems with the lien itself, such as the fraudulent transfer laws and tax concerns. This complexity creates a two-edged sword. To succeed takes knowledge and skill in several different legal areas. The costs involved can be significant when you include the legal fees, taxes and special business services – such as international managers. Yet, executed properly, the complexity of the transaction can impose a formidable barrier against the average plaintiff seeking a fast lawsuit recovery. As more Americans become concerned about lawsuits, and as they more fully educate themselves about asset protection, there will be increased demand for these more sophisticated protective strategies. Third party mortgage arrangements to protect investment properties and other assets will be high on that list.

If I equity-strip or lien my properties; how do I shield the loan proceeds?

Protecting the cash proceeds from borrowing against your properties is far easier than structuring the mortgages. You wouldn't normally equity-strip your properties until you're in crisis mode and foresee a judgment. Only then would you complete the loan and transfer the proceeds together with your other liquid assets to an international protective entity. Or you might convert the proceeds to exempt assets. We wouldn't use limited partnerships, LLCs or other domestic entities to shelter the loan proceeds because at that point in time such transfers would be susceptible to fraudulent transfer claims.

However it's structured, the ultimate gameplan, once in a crisis mode, is to transfer your domestic (U.S.-based) assets to protective entities (i.e., FLPs, LLCs, corporations, etc.) *and* fully secure your assets to mortgage holders so there is little or no equity exposed. You then transfer the loan proceeds to an international trust, international LLC, self-protected investment (i.e. international annuities) or through all or some of these layered entities and firewalls.

What other strategies can be used to reduce the equity in investment real estate?

There are endless strategies. For example, you may try to depress the value of your property so it has less equity susceptible to creditors. For instance, you might give purchase options to 'insiders,' or decontrolled entities to purchase the property at about 70 percent of fair market value. This probably would not be a fraudulent transfer. The option holder then has first claim to the property at the option price which defeats the creditor's rights to claim the full equity. Of course, the option must be timely recorded before the creditor's attachment, but this arrangement will depress the property's value by eliminating the 30 percent equity otherwise claimable by the creditor. Or, as another example, you may assign your rents to a third party as security for a loan. That will impede the creditor's rights to the cash flow. There are many more possibilities.

How can I reduce my personal exposure from managing the properties in my LLCs?

Property owners are smart to consider this point. While they have no personal liability for the contracts and debts of the LLC; they can nevertheless be personally sued, together with the LLC, for their personal acts of negligence in managing the LLC – or any other entity for that matter.

Real estate, particularly investment and rental properties, creates enormous liabilities ranging from breach of lease, to 'slip and fall', to environmental and toxic waste claims. This is a major reason to title your commercial properties to an LLC, as the manager generally has no personal responsibility for the debts of the LLC. Nevertheless, the LLC should carry adequate liability insurance. Many of our clients form another LLC or corporation to manage the LLC that owns their property. This further distances them from potential personal liability as property managers.

In sum, you want to shield yourself from both 'outside-in' and 'inside-out' liability. 'Outside-in' means that your ownership of the property cannot be claimed by your personal creditors. 'Inside-out' insulates you and your personal assets from liabilities arising from your owning or managing the property.

6

Protecting

Your

Investments

Now that you explained how one may shield their residence and other real estate, let's go on to talk about protecting one's cash and liquid investments.

How unsafe is it for spouses to own their investments (savings, CDs, stocks, bonds, mutual funds, etc) in their individual names?

Obviously, it's the most dangerous way to title these important assets. Yet many people who own considerable investments do title their accounts in their individual names. Or the spouses may own their investments jointly. But either form of ownership leaves these assets unprotected. You never want to keep these assets in your own name. They should always be titled to a protective entity unless they are exempt or protected by state or federal law.

What is the best way to protectively title investments and other liquid assets?

Here you have several good options. One option is to title your cash, CDs, mutual funds and other liquid investments to one or more limited partnerships (LPs). We most frequently use LPs to protect liquid investments because; 1) the LP lets you control these assets; 2) your LP interest cannot be claimed by your creditors; 3) the LP is tax-neutral; 4) the LP gives you maximum ownership and operating flexibility; and 5) the LP lets you better plan your estate and reduce your estate taxes. The LP is both versatile and protective. Most comprehensive asset protection plans include at least one limited partnership. But the limited partnership is only one option. Some planners recommend limited liability companies (LLCs) because they too are COPES (limiting creditors only to the charging order). But we prefer the limited partnership for these assets because the limited partnership is designed to own 'safe' assets and the LLC is preferable for business purposes and to own non-residential real estate. Moreover, the limited partnership provides for discounted estate tax valuations and finally, the limited partnership can simultaneously own the client's multiple LLCs or C corporations and thus serve as the foundation for their entire plan.

Some clients use domestic trusts to hold their investments. Revocable living trusts are not recommended to own these assets because they provide no protection. On the other hand, irrevocable trusts require you to relinquish control and beneficial enjoyment of these assets. Domestic asset protection trusts (DAPTs) can be self-settled; that is the settlor can also be a beneficiary. However, DAPTs have their own limitations and restrictions. We will discuss this when we talk about estate protection. There are, of course, other options, but these are the most typical ways to protect investments.

Which is your best option? That depends upon your personal situation, the value of these assets, your estate plan, and your financial and tax objectives. That's why you should involve your financial planner, tax advisor and insurance professional in your planning. You not only want to protect these assets, but also structure them correctly considering your other goals. Remember, your financial professionals are important members of your wealth protection team and they are essential to a coordinated, integrated plan.

Since you strongly suggest the limited partnership to protect liquid investments, can you give me an overview of the limited partnership?

A limited partnership has one or more *general partners* and one or more *limited partners*. The general partner(s) have the same rights and liabilities of a partner in a general partnership – they manage the partnership and have unlimited liability for partnership debts. The limited partners have very limited rights to participate in the management of the partnership. They cannot play an active role in managing the partnership. Their liability is also limited to their investment in the partnership, as limited partners aren't personally liable for partnership debts. As owners of the partnership, the partnership income or losses pass directly to them for tax purposes. The family limited partnership (FLP) is a limited partnership that only has family members as partners. Ordinarily, the husband and wife are the general partners and they control the FLP. The family limited partnership's limited partnership interest may be owned by the parents, other family members, or by other family controlled entities, such as one or more trusts or LLCs. You can easily restructure an FLP to maximize your lawsuit protection, minimize estate taxes and achieve other estate planning objectives.

What assets can the limited partnership own and what assets should it not own?

The LP is an excellent vehicle to safeguard savings, CDs, money market funds, mutual funds, stocks, bonds, REIT interests, C corporation shares, limited liability company memberships and even limited partnership interests in other limited partnerships. The LP cannot own S corporation shares. It should not own annuities (which may then lose their tax deferral). Retirement accounts or special accounts – such as 529 plans – should usually remain outside the LP. Moreover, an LP shouldn't own liability-producing assets such as real estate, equipment or vehicles since the LP's general partners are personally liable for lawsuits arising from its assets. That's why it's preferable to title your 'dangerous' assets to a limited liability company. And as we said earlier, the family home should generally not be owned by a limited partnership.

While transfers of assets to a limited partnership generally have no tax consequence, it is always wisest to check with your accountant about the tax consequences before you title any asset to a limited partnership – or any other entity.

How can we most defensively structure our limited partnership?

There are a number of interesting possibilities. For example, the limited partners can allocate their ownership interests or profit distributions as they elect. This is important for protection. For instance, you can contribute your personal assets to the partnership for a proportionately smaller partnership share and the remaining limited partnership interest can be owned by other family members. However, that's a taxable gift if the other family members are not your spouse. Again, it's important that your accountant review your limited partnership's proposed structure to avoid tax liability and also to determine that the LP is favorable from a tax standpoint.

Families adopt rather typical limited partnership structures. For example, mom and dad may form the LP and contribute various income-producing investments in exchange for their partnership interests. As the general partners, they may each receive a two percent partnership interest. As the general partners, they would equally control the partnership, much as they jointly controlled the contributed assets. As the limited partners, mom and dad would own the remaining 96 percent limited partnership interest. (General and limited partners can be the same parties.) Under this arrangement, mom and dad would now exclusively and equally own and control the partnership and its assets. You see, there's no real change from when their assets were titled to their individual or joint names – only now their assets are protected.

There are other structural possibilities. If dad has creditors, mom may become the sole general partner. Or mom and dad may form a corporation or LLC to be the general partner. This is a particularly good arrangement if the partnership can incur liabilities for which the general partners would have liability. Using a corporation or LLC as the general partner also adds privacy as to those personally involved in the entity.

You can easily modify limited partnership structures. For instance, one spouse may eventually own a greater partnership interest, or parents may gradually gift their limited partnership interests to their children, to their living trusts, or to other entities. The limited partnership's flexibility works especially well for estate planning and lifetime gifting.

How does a limited partnership protect investments?

It works in much the same way that an LLC protects assets. A limited partnership is a COPE or charging order protected entity. A limited or general partner's creditor cannot seize the debtor's limited partnership interest. The judgment creditor can only have the court issue a charging order against the debtor's limited partnership interest. The charging order gives the creditor only the right to profits or liquidation proceeds actually paid to the limited partner. As with the LLC, the charging order creditor doesn't become a substitute partner. Nor does the creditor gain other partnership rights, other than the right to profits or distributions payable to the debtor-partner. For example, the partner's creditor cannot sell or auction the partnership interest or vote as a limited partner. Nor can the creditor inspect the partnership books. The creditor becomes only a limited assignee of the limited partnership interest, and only for purposes of collecting profits or distributions voted by the general partners and actually distributable to the limited partner.

And as with the LLC, the reason the partner's personal creditor is restricted to the limited charging order remedy is to protect the partners uninvolved in the debts of the debtor-partner. The objective is to prevent a partner's personal creditors from unduly interfering in the affairs of the partnership. In contrast, a corporate shareholder's personal creditors can claim the debtor-shareholder's shares. They then become a successor stockholder, with all the rights of a stockholder. For these reasons the LP or LLC are so useful in our planning to safeguard personal wealth.

Because the creditor's right to distributed profits or liquidating proceeds due the debtor-partner is the creditor's sole remedy, you might ask how effective that remedy is. Consider its limitations. Partnership profits can be illusive, particularly when the limited partnership is family-owned and the interests of the partners are closely aligned – as is true with most limited partnerships. Second, the decision to distribute profits belongs exclusively to the general partners. A member's creditor cannot force distributions. A limited partnership can then defer profit distributions until the charging order creditor loses patience and favorably settles. This deferred distribution strategy deprives the debtor-partner from ever receiving partnership funds subject to seizure. However, in the interim, the debtor-partner can accept loans, salaries, consulting fees or payments for other assets sold to the limited partnership. The debtor-partner also has a number of legal ways to divert profits to other family entities that may transact business with the limited partnership and can thus be a protective conduit for the partnership earnings. These distributed funds would not be subject to the charging order because they are not distributed profits from the limited partnership. Interestingly, you can also structure your limited partnership to allocate a greater portion of profits to non-debtor partners who may own a proportionately smaller partnership interest. For example, you can own 90 percent of the limited partnership and, by agreement, be entitled to only 10 percent or less of its profits. You can see there are many opportunities to defeat a charging order creditor.

We generally don't want a debtor-partner to be a general partner because we would not want a court to order him to make profit distributions, which is altogether possible if the same debtor-partner is a significant limited partner. Oftentimes it is advisable to set up an international LLC to be the general partner. International LLC managers further insulate the LP management from U.S. court directives.

But if I do own a limited partnership interest in a limited partnership but do not control the profit distributions, couldn't I then lose those profit distributions?

It's true that you can't as easily frustrate a creditor when you own a minority interest in a limited partnership that has outside investors and an unaffiliated general partner whose interests and agenda don't necessarily coincide with your own as the debtor-partner. Should the partnership generate and distribute substantial profits, the charging order creditor would receive your distributions. The debtor-partner's option then is to sell or encumber his partnership interest, or alternatively title the limited partnership interest to another protected entity, such as another limited partnership that would be under the control of the debtor-partner.

How frequently do a limited partner's creditors obtain charging orders?

That's the bottom line question. Surprisingly few creditors apply for charging orders – and for one good reason: The charging order creditor can become liable for federal taxes due on the partnership profits earned by the debtor-partner, even if the creditor never receives profit distributions from the partnership. Consider the creditor with a charging order against a limited partner who owns a 50 percent partnership interest. If the partnership earns $100,000 a year, the 50 percent debtor-partner pays income taxes on $50,000 as 'pass-through' income. Instead, the charging order creditor assumes the partner's tax liability, even if the creditor received no distribution. Therefore, a creditor in a 35 percent tax bracket would pay a $17,500 tax each year the charging order is in effect, assuming the partnership generates the same profits. So if there are undistributed profits, the creditor has only a tax liability. And several states prevent a charging order creditor from releasing their charging order without the consent of the debtor-partner. A debtor-partner with taxable income from the partnership may understandably withhold this consent. You can see how the charging order can easily become a liability rather than a way to recover on a judgment. The shift of tax liability from the debtor-partner to his charging order creditor is true only in certain circumstances that are too technical to detail here; but a good asset protection attorney can usually structure the limited partnership so that the possibility of the creditor incurring a large tax debt becomes a real deterrent to a creditor pursuing the charging order.

Can the limited partnership also protect against divorce?

Yes. A correctly structured LP can provide *some* protection against divorce. For instance, the LP agreement may provide that if divorce forces an involuntary transfer of an LP interest to the spouse, the other partners may have first option to buy the LP interest for an amount less than the underlying value of the LP assets. But you must carefully draft LP agreements for this purpose. Also, if one spouse is the sole general partner before the divorce, and owns 50 percent of the LP after the divorce, then the other spouse cannot remove that spouse as the general partner. Thus, the general partner spouse would continue to control the LP assets, notwithstanding that the LP is equally owned with the ex-spouse.

Is it too late to transfer my investments to a limited partnership once I've been sued?

No, but the limited partnership may then not adequately protect you. The reason is that your creditor might ignore the charging order remedy and instead attempt to set aside the transfer of your assets to the limited partnership as a fraudulent transfer. The assets would then be unprotected and subject to creditor seizure. This is a far more threatening possibility than a charging order. Creditors can recover assets fraudulently transferred to limited partnerships or any other entity. Of course, a partner's personal creditor cannot directly claim the limited partnership assets because these assets no longer belong to the debtor-partner; they are owned instead by the limited partnership.

However, the outcome of these cases chiefly depends on how you structure your limited partnership. For instance, if you and your wife each contribute equally to the limited partnership, and each receives in exchange an equal partnership interest, then the court may consider this to be a 'fair consideration' transfer and not fraudulent because you each now own one-half of the limited partnership. But, if you and your spouse contribute equally and you receive something less than a 50 percent partnership interest, you essentially 'gave away' assets and its value could be recovered by your present creditors. Still, receiving an ownership interest that is proportionate to your contributed capital doesn't guarantee that a court won't still set aside the transfer once you have a present creditor. Courts have ruled that impairing a present creditor from collection is sufficient for a transfer to be fraudulent – even when the consideration (the limited partnership interests) equals the value of the assets transferred. Since the law on this point is not settled you cannot assume that transfers to a limited partnership are safe *after* you have a creditor. This again underscores why it's so important to lawsuit-proof yourself *before* you incur liabilities. To solve this potential problem we oftentimes use international entities that are considerably more protective than the limited partnership.

Some asset protection attorneys suggest using an international trust to be the limited partner of a limited partnership. Do you agree?

In many cases we do. For maximum protection, it's best to have your limited partnership interest owned by an international asset protection trust. Under this arrangement, family members can be the general partners and control the partnership and its assets until a creditor threatens the partnership or its assets when the partnership can liquidate its assets. If an international trust owns, say 98 percent of the partnership, and serious trouble strikes, the international trust would receive 98 percent of the liquidated partnership assets. The partnership proceeds now internationally would be considerably better protected. Moreover, if an international trust owns the limited partnership, it is not subject to charging orders arising from claims against family members. The limited partnership/international trust is almost a standard arrangement for more significant wealth protection plans. We will talk more about international entities to protect cash assets.

Are there other ways to maximize one's limited partnership protection?

You can use a number of different strategies to bolster your limited partnership protection. For example, your limited partnership agreement might: 1) give the general partners full discretion to withhold profit distributions; 2) the partnership agreement can specifically restrict the transfer of a limited partnership interest without the consent of the general partner, and/or all or a majority of the limited partners; 3) the agreement may further prevent a limited partner from withdrawing capital contributions without unanimous partner consent; 4) the agreement may also specify that a creditor of a limited partner becomes only an assignee of the limited partner's interest and acquires absolutely no partnership rights other than rights to distributions; 5) the limited partnership agreement can further allow the general partner to 'assess' the limited partners for further contributions. This obligation should expressly extend to charging order creditors. 6) 'High-risk' family members might own a smaller partnership interest or be entitled to a proportionately smaller share of the income; 7) spouses may title their limited partnership interests as tenants-by-the-entirety – if their state creditor protects this tenancy type. This protects the partnership interest from creditor claims against one spouse. 8) Finally, if you do invest in a non-controlled limited partnership or limited liability company, you may title your ownership interest to a family limited partnership that you *do* control. This will protect your profit distributions. A well-drafted limited partnership agreement can create a formidable creditor barrier. An asset protection attorney would know how to optimize the protection from a limited partnership. As a final protective measure, you can encumber or lien your partnership interest or its underlying assets so the secured creditor has first claim to profit distributions before the charging order creditor.

What are the limited partnership's tax ramifications?

Another major advantage of limited partnerships, which also extend to multi-member LLCs, is the partnership tax treatment. When compared to the corporation or sole proprietorship, the more notable partnership tax benefits are: First, subject to certain restrictions, partners may distribute partnership income, gain, loss, or credit among the partners however they see fit. In other words, one partner may contribute little or no capital to the partnership, but receive a disproportionately larger share of partnership gain or loss, along with the tax benefits or liabilities associated with this. Compare this to a corporation, where a stockholder may only receive company profits in proportion to the amount of shares they own.

Secondly, within certain limits, a partnership may distribute appreciated or depreciated property to a partner without recognizing gain or loss. For example, let's say an individual bought a lot of raw land for $10,000. Ten years later he contributed it to the partnership, and eight years after that it was redistributed to its original owner. At the time of distribution, the property's value had appreciated to $100,000. If the distribution had been made from a C or S corporation, the company (and also the shareholder, in the case of a C corporation) would have to recognize gain of $90,000, which means it would have to pay capital gains tax on $90,000 gain. Since there is no recognition of gain with a partnership in this instance, there is no requirement to revalue the property or pay the tax.

Thirdly, any partner may make additional contributions of appreciated property to a partnership at any time without recognizing gain on the property. A new partner may also likewise make a contribution to an existing partnership without recognizing gain. If such contributions were made to a C or S corporation, however, a gain would be recognized unless the contributor belonged to a group who, collectively, owned at least 80 percent of the partnership. Recognizing gain, of course, is a term that means you have to pay capital gains tax to the extent your property appreciated in value.

Fourth, distributions to limited partners are not subject to the self-employment tax, which can be quite burdensome. Although C and S corporation distributions are also not subject to self-employment taxes; general partnerships and sole proprietorship profits are usually subject to this tax. Note that a general partner's interest in an LP may still be subject to self-employment taxes, however this exposure is often reduced by giving the general partner a smaller (1 percent or so) interest in the company (the general partner's management salary, however, is still subject to self-employment or the equivalent FICA/FUTA taxes).

Fifth, when a partnership partially or completely buys out a partner's interest, the remaining partners receive a step-up in basis of that partner's share; to the extent that partner recognized gain. In layman's terms, this means that the bought-out partnership interest, and the capital connected to it, is re-valued to its current fair market value without triggering capital gains tax. If the partner's interest is sold for more than what it was worth when he bought into the partnership, the partner will recognize gain, but the partnership will receive the step-up. Corporations do not receive this benefit, meaning that even if a shareholder sells his company interest for a profit, gain (with no tax break) will still be recognized when appreciated company assets are distributed. This step-up in basis also occurs if a partnership interest is transferred due to a third party purchase, death of a partner, or otherwise.

Sixth, in some circumstances, partnership losses may be used to offset the individual tax liabilities of each partner, and as we'll discuss later, limited partnerships may be used to reduce estate tax liability while passing company interests tax-free to one's heirs. These tax reduction strategies are not available to C or S corporations, general partnerships or sole proprietorships.

Although there are many benefits to partnership taxation, there are instances where other tax classifications are more desirable, or where partnership taxation is a hindrance rather than a benefit. However, most tax advisors consider partnership tax law to be the most favorable, in most circumstances, both to the entity and its owners.

What if we are heavily invested in a business that is a C corporation? How can we lawsuit-proof our stock ownership in our C corporation?

The family business is often the family's major asset, and frequently, it is a C corporation. But even if it is a public corporation, you must protectively title these corporate shares. If these shares are owned by you individually, they can be seized by your creditors. You should instead title these shares to a family limited partnership (FLP). For example, a husband and wife (or either spouse) as the general partners would control the partnership. In turn, the LP owns and controls the stock interest in the corporation. Or you may title the corporate shares to an irrevocable trust. Your children, for instance, can be the beneficiaries. The husband and wife as co-trustees of the trust can then manage the trust that controls the corporation. In either instance, the spouses would indirectly control the corporate assets without directly owning the corporate shares. Another option is to title the shares to an international trust. It well-protects corporate shares. Or you may title your shares with your spouse as tenants-by-the-entirety if your state protects T/E shares against one spouse's creditors. Obviously, you can also pledge or encumber your shares to a friendly creditor as you can any other asset.

But you do raise an important point. Many people do not think about protecting their stock ownership in their own business – and frequently this is both their major asset and a C corporation. If their shareholder interest in their own business is exposed, it's poor business and personal planning.

For protection, why can't I simply title my investments – cash, stocks, etc. – to a corporation?

We wouldn't recommend a corporation to protect your personal assets. As we say, if you directly own the corporate shares, your shares can be claimed by your creditors. That's why you must layer your protection using a trust, limited partnership or some other protective entity to own the corporate shares. You may also have holding company tax consequences when you title your personal investments to a corporation. The limited partnership or LLC is the far better alternative to a corporation to protect your personal assets.

How can we make our stock less attractive to prospective litigants?

The answer is to protectively title your corporate shares to a limited partnership or some other entity. But you have other tactics available that can reduce the value of your corporate shares to a creditor. For example, you may: 1) issue irrevocable proxies which assign your right to vote your shares. If you issue a proxy to a relative, for example, a creditor who seizes your shares can't vote your shares since you have irrevocably assigned your voting rights to your proxy holder. If the creditor gains no voting rights, it significantly lessens the stock's value to the creditor (depending upon the importance of voting control). You can also sometimes exchange voting shares for non-voting shares, which similarly lessens the stock's value. 2) You may also allow the corporation to assess your shares. Corporate shares assessable by the corporation are unattractive to a creditor because the creditor assumes the assessment. A potentially large assessment by the corporation correspondingly lowers the shares value to your creditors. 3) Another possibility is to dilute your stock ownership. Why allow your creditor to control your family business? You can sell additional shares to other family members, or to family controlled entities (trusts, limited partnerships, etc.) to prevent your creditor from gaining control over the corporation. Or you may redeem your shares. As another example, you may title your shares to an irrevocable trust. Finally, you may pledge your shares as collateral for loans. Of course, you can use these tactics in any combination. What is the best way to protect, redeem, transfer or encumber your shares, will, of course, depend on the corporate restrictions and your personal situation.

What is the best way to protect S corporation shares?

It is far more difficult to protect S corporation shares than C corporation shares. That is one disadvantage to the S corporation. Although C corporation shares can be protectively titled to limited partnerships, irrevocable trusts or other entities; these methods are, unfortunately, unavailable to protect S corporation shares. S corporations cannot be owned by these entities or the corporation will lose its S corporation election. It is then far more difficult to lawsuit-proof S corporation shares because of its ownership restrictions. However, S corporations can be owned by single-member domestic or international LLCs (which are taxed as disregarded entities). S corporation shares can also be owned by a sub-trust of an international asset protection trust – although this arrangement is more complex. Another option is to title S corporation shares to a husband and wife as tenants-by-the-entirety if

106

their state T/E laws are sufficiently protective. Finally, for protection, you may encumber or pledge your S corporation shares as you would encumber C corporation shares or any other asset. Again, the method we use in any given case depends on the circumstances.

I heard that it is safer to keep investment accounts in a state other than where you reside? Do you agree?

That can be a good idea for this reason. To enforce their judgment against your assets, your creditor must obtain a judgment in the state where your assets are located. When your assets are located in another state, your creditor must obtain a judgment from that state to seize those assets. Courts in one state cannot seize property in another state. Relocating your liquid assets to other states can thus delay or frustrate a creditor attempting collection. But, obviously, this is seldom a good long-term strategy – though it can delay seizure of your investments until you develop a more formidable plan. In any event, you want to title these accounts to a protective entity – such as an FLP or LLC in another state. Also, for maximum safety, keep these accounts in banks or brokerage firms whose offices are outside your own state. These steps are unnecessary in most situations but we have recommended these strategies in some instances.

Can one entity – say an LLC – hold all my assets, including my investments?

An axiom of good asset protection planning is to title your investments and other 'safe assets' to one entity, such as a limited partnership, and title such dangerous or liability-producing assets as vehicles, equipment, real estate or businesses to other separate entities – usually one, or multiple LLCs. Why jeopardize your valuable or 'safe' assets to the creditors and lawsuits that arise from your dangerous or liability-producing assets? That's your gamble when you title all your assets to one entity. You always want to limit your exposure. That's why you should isolate your liability-prone assets to separate entities and title your safe assets to another.

For privacy and protection, do you recommend owning bearer investments?

We do not provide investment advice, but owning bearer investments do provide more privacy. Gold, diamonds, art, stamp collections, coins and collectibles are self-protective to the extent they're easily stored or transported internationally, and their ownership is confidential and private. For more privacy, you can buy and sell these collectibles through a third party – such as an international entity. Gold or diamonds occupy little space, and can be converted to cash with confidentiality and privacy. Private vaults in international countries provide even more secrecy. But do pay your taxes on any profits from these investments. Also own these assets through an international protective entity such as an international trust or LLC to add privacy and enhance protection. Of course, you must decide whether these are suitable investments for you.

I hear a lot of Americans have their money internationally. Is international asset protection legal? Safe?

For the safest protection you should keep a portion of your assets in an international jurisdiction. International family wealth planning has been popular for 2,000 years, originating with the Roman emperors who relocated their fortunes to international lands to preserve their riches for their descendants. International wealth protection is far more popular today, primarily because of our lawsuit explosion. Trillions are now protected in various international financial centers (IFCs) whose asset protection laws attract wealth from less-protective countries. Each year we find more Americans seeking international asset protection and international investing opportunities. They realize that 'going international' can be the safest place for their money in these unsafe times. Unfortunately, one of the impediments we have to sound asset protection planning is the client – or their ill-informed advisors – who nonsensically believe shifting wealth internationally is somehow illegal, unsafe or only for tax evaders, money-launders or other assorted criminals. That's why we frequently have to re-educate our clients or their advisors on the benefits of international planning. But as we say, education is a major part of what we do.

How do international financial centers (IFCs) protect wealth?

There are many reasons why international asset protection is so effective. One reason, for example, is that international asset protection centers don't enforce U.S. judgments or judicial or administrative orders. You thus gain jurisdictional immunity. Countries that won't enforce U.S. *civil* decrees are the countries we use for lawsuit protection. Since these countries don't recognize American judgments or civil decrees, the creditor must re-litigate their case within that international jurisdiction. For many reasons, this may be impractical or impossible. For instance, the statute of limitations may have expired, or the country may not recognize the type liability which is the basis for the lawsuit. These countries also impose procedural obstacles to effectively blockade creditors and litigation. Asset protection jurisdictions are debtor-friendly. They're in business to protect their customers' wealth. Wealth protection is what they sell. And they do it well.

Asset protection jurisdictions make their protective entities even *more* protective than do other countries. International asset protection trusts, limited liability companies, limited partnerships, foundations, captive insurance companies, international business companies, hybrid companies and various other entities, each provide considerably better protection than do comparable U.S. entities. That's why few judgment creditors recover a defendant's international wealth. Without their international protection, many debtors would undoubtedly have lost their money. And contrary to myth, it's perfectly legal to invest and protect your money internationally. Nor is it difficult or unsafe. But you must do it correctly. For instance, you must comply with the IRS reporting requirements and pay the taxes on your international earnings. You want to go international either for creditor protection or

109

to invest. You *don't* go international to save taxes. Most international protective arrangements are tax-neutral and will neither reduce, defer nor increase your taxes.

How can I learn more about safeguarding my money internationally?

You want to become knowledgeable! It builds confidence, and confidence prompts action. That's why we educate our clients. It builds their confidence. Your own international program will proceed and function more smoothly once you fully understand the process. There's also no substitute for good professional advice.

What assets can I protect internationally?

You can protect virtually your entire net worth internationally. Cash, securities and collectibles (gold and jewelry) and other assets that you can physically relocate internationally are ideal. Real estate, cars, boats, U.S. securities and other U.S.-based assets necessarily remain within the jurisdiction and recovery powers of the U.S. courts and generally are not transferred to international entities. The trustees, protectors and other fiduciaries who control your assets internationally would be international firms who remain beyond the control and recovery powers of the American courts. But to fully lawsuit-proof yourself, you would shift as much of your wealth as possible internationally. For example, you can directly transfer your liquid assets internationally, and then mortgage or sell your U.S.-based assets and invest the cash proceeds internationally. Your creditors' only recourse then through the U.S. courts is to seize your equity-stripped assets which would then have little or no value to your creditor. You thus *constructively* shift your total net worth internationally though you may still own significant assets *domestically*.

Is the international asset protection trust (IAPT) the best entity for international assets?

The international asset protection trust (IAPT) is the traditional protective entity. It became popular in the 1980s because of the escalating need and demand for lawsuit

110

protection. But international trusts can be used for other purposes: To avoid forced heirship laws, for premarital planning, estate planning or international business planning. The international trust compares to domestic irrevocable trusts, though for many reasons, the international trust is considerably more protective. The primary reason is that the international trust is *foreign*. That one difference is critical. U.S. trusts are *always* vulnerable to creditors and creditor friendly U.S. courts. The IAPT is immune. Debtor friendly international financial centers govern their enforcement. U.S. court orders to repatriate the trust assets are ignored by international trustees. Your trust funds *won't* be returned for the benefit of your creditor. Moreover, the trustee can relocate your trust and its assets to another jurisdiction if your trust becomes endangered. The trustee can also withhold distributions to beneficiaries with creditors. Aside from these enormously protective features, the IAPT compares to the U.S. irrevocable trust. The international trust has a *grantor* (or settlor, donor or trustor) who creates and funds the trust, appoints the trustees and protector, and names the beneficiaries. The *trustee* manages the trust for the beneficiaries. The *beneficiaries* receive the trust's income and/or assets. The IAPT's *protector* oversees and can replace the trustee, and approves major trustee actions. Finally, you can create self-settled trusts internationally and be a beneficiary of your own trust. Excepting for domestic asset protection trusts – available in only a few states, self-settled trusts provide no creditor protection. This final point is important. Only DAPT states provide creditor protection for self-settled trusts – or a trust where the grantor is also a beneficiary.

Which are the best international jurisdictions?
You can form international trusts in a number of international financial centers. Nevis, the Cook Islands, Cayman Islands, Belize, Isle of Man, the Bahamas, and the Turks and Caicos Islands are popular choices. Nevis and the Cook Islands, in our view, are the two most protective IFCs. Where you set up your trust is chiefly based on the legal protection afforded by that IFC; however, you would not necessarily bank or invest within that jurisdiction since you can globally invest the money in your trust. Lawsuit protection can open the door to new, more profitable international

investments.

Are international LLCs more protective than domestic LLCs?

The Nevis and Cook Island LLCs are both significantly more protective than domestic LLCs. As with the domestic LLC, a judgment creditor of an international LLC's member is limited to a charging order against that debtor member's profit distributions. Moreover, with the Nevis LLC, the creditor pays U.S. taxes on earnings attributable to the debtor-member from the Nevis LLC – even if earnings were not distributed by the Nevis LLC. This is the same with a domestic LLC. Moreover, the member's creditor cannot claim the member's interest in the LLC, nor replace its management. Most significantly, Nevis LLC law prevents a present creditor from pursuing fraudulent transfer claims against the debtor's assets transferred to the Nevis LLC provided the debtor exchanged the contributed assets for a proportionate ownership interest in the LLC. This is not necessarily so with domestic LLCs. You have other advantages with the international LLC. The international LLC as a disregarded entity requires some but minimal IRS reporting. Moreover, the Nevis LLC can be flexibly structured to achieve virtually any asset protection, estate planning, business or investment objective. The Nevis LLC, for U.S. tax purposes, can elect to be taxed either as a C corporation or partnership. Officers and directors of the Nevis LLC are personally immune from the LLCs liabilities. The Nevis or Cook Islands LLCs are excellent alternatives for those who want good protection internationally at less cost than forming an IAPT. You won't save U.S. taxes with the Nevis LLC or any other international entity, as American taxpayers must report and pay US taxes on all international earnings in the year the income was earned.

When would an international trust be preferable to the international LLC for international protection?

The IAPT and international LLC each have their place in our planning. Nor is it a matter that one entity is better than the other. Each has its advantages and applications. For estate planning, we naturally would use the trust as the entity of choice. But to shield smaller sums of money we may opt for the international LLC. Most often, we use both the IAPT and the international LLC to layer our protection. The IAPT owns the international LLC and invests and transacts business through the LLC. This is a fairly common arrangement.

When would someone use an international entity – such as a Nevis LLC – rather than a domestic or U.S. entity?

You'd go international whenever you question whether your domestic plan will adequately protect you. An instance would be when a *present* creditor might ignore the charging order remedy and attempt to set aside an asset transfer to a domestic limited partnership, LLC or domestic trust. It's poor planning if your creditor can argue that your transfer was fraudulent. You are then safer with transfers to a Nevis LLC because Nevis expressly deems these transfers *not* fraudulent. In this respect, a properly structured Nevis LLC is more protective than the international trust – particularly when you already have creditors. Transfers to the trust could be a fraudulent conveyance and contestable in the trust's jurisdiction, although practical obstacles may still prevent creditor recovery. This deserves repeating. If a Nevis LLC member has an *existing* creditor, Nevis LLC laws allow the member to transfer his or her assets to the LLC without it being *a fraudulent conveyance* if the debtor-member's interest is proportionate to his share of the contributed capital. This transfer is considered a fair value exchange and not fraudulent. Interestingly, a promise of a future investment in the Nevis LLC by a present or incoming LLC member can be used to measure this proportionality. A debtor-member can then own a minority interest, subject to the charging order, though the debtor-member contributed all or most of the LLC's present assets – provided the majority member contractually promised to pay its larger proportional share later. This dilution strategy can effectively discourage creditors whose charging order recourse is then only against only a small minority interest in the LLC. This feature is unique to the Nevis LLC. It's only one example of how we can achieve safer results internationally.

Are international trusts and LLCs the only two protective entities?

The IAPT and international LLCs are the two most commonly used international entities. However, we have many other options. For example, some international financial centers feature hybrid companies and companies limited by guarantee; each with their own protective twists: Their owners don't directly own their shares. Panama and Lichtenstein foundations somewhat compare to international trusts. Bahamian limited partnerships closely parallel U.S. limited partnerships. As with U.S. entities, the international entities protection comes through different features and mechanisms.

If I do put my money internationally do I lose access to my money?

As the grantor of an IAPT you cannot revoke the trust, but if you're not under court duress, you can access the trust funds. For example, as a trust beneficiary you can borrow from the trust, or you can collateralize loans to yourself through 'back-to-back' financing. Your trust might also transact business with you or your company, and in that manner 'indirectly' conduit funds to you. The trustee can distribute funds to any beneficiary, including yourself if you are a beneficiary. If you're not a beneficiary, your spouse and/or children are likely to be. There are many ways to quickly access your international funds. There are even ways to make your trust revocable with the assent of *both* the trustee and the protector. But as the grantor, you cannot solely exercise the right to revoke or control your trust or access your assets, or you'll lose your protection.

These issues of control, repatriation of their international funds and other practical considerations are – and should be – foremost in the minds of our international clients. Again, our role is to carefully explain to our clients how these entities work in practice so they fully understand what to expect. The asset protection attorney who does not fully inform the client does the client a disservice.

I have read that some international trusts have failed. Are they really as protective as you say?

The real question is – what is more protective? It's true that your international trust won't be effective for protection unless your trust is structured and administered properly. And there have been a few celebrated cases where international trusts have failed. Those few cases highlight one or more fatal mistakes that you must avoid. In one or two cases the grantor retained too much control, which allowed the court to determine that the trust was nothing more than a sham. For protection, you must give your trustee complete control over your trust – not only in form, but also in practice. In other cases the trust assets were held within the U.S. where they could then be seized by a U.S. court when the transfer to the trust was deemed fraudulent. You must keep your assets internationally. In other cases the trust lacked necessary protective safeguards, or the trust was technically defective. For these reasons, you need your trust prepared by an experienced professional.

In some of these cases, the grantor was ordered by the court to repatriate the trust assets for the benefit of the creditor. When the grantor failed or refused to do so, he was jailed for contempt. These rulings were proper in at least those cases where the grantor had *defacto* control over their trust. In other instances, the trust was set up only days before the court proceeding. But ordinarily, a court cannot find you in contempt for your failure to repatriate your money if you truly lack the power to comply with the court order, which a properly structured and administered trust should accomplish. Moreover, your trust shouldn't appear to be a last minute effort to put your assets beyond the court's reach.

Timing and relinquishing control are both vital to international success. That's why you can't wait until the last moment to protect yourself. You want to set up your international entities well before you have a liability, or at least before you are sued. And don't try to control your trust so the court won't reasonably conclude that you have the power to repatriate the trust funds. You are less likely to make these mistakes if your trust is overseen by an attorney experienced with international trusts and the rulings in these recent cases. Still, exceptionally few international trusts are challenged and instances where a creditor recovered money from international entities are even more rare. That's why we began our answer to your question with our own question – what is the safer option than an international strategy? If the litigation skies are clear, buying exempt assets or domestic entities may afford you equally sound protection, but once the storm clouds gather, we know of nothing safer than a well-constructed international fortress.

If I'm sued, can't I simply hide my international cash in an international bank account?

International banking records are normally privacy protected against U.S. court orders and subpoenas, and international financial centers banks are jurisdictionally immune to service of process. IFC's banks cannot divulge your financial information to third parties except as permitted under narrow treaty provisions. Because international banks are jurisdictionally immune to service of process, they can also ban U.S. writs of execution or attachment orders. The secrecy laws of most IFCs can protect funds from creditor seizure originating from a U.S. judgment. They can also protect the confidentiality of financial transactions passing through the bank. Still, you need a protective entity – such as an international trust or international LLC – to protect yourself against a U.S. turnover or disgorgement order. Creditors may discover your international accounts. Nor can you refuse to disclose them under discovery processes, if you are asked about them. Finally, the existence of these accounts must be reported to the IRS, and this information may be obtained by your creditor. Concealing or hiding is never a good protective strategy!

Let's return for a moment to the question of taxes and tax reporting. How does 'going international' affect taxes?

We emphasize to our clients that they cannot save taxes internationally. Certain IRS qualified international annuities and life insurance products can legally defer taxes – as can their U.S. counterparts – but as a general rule all international income is reportable to the IRS as taxable income in the year earned, not the year it's repatriated to the U.S. We instruct our clients to immediately notify their accountant whenever we set up international structures so the client and their accountant can do the necessary tax reporting.

If I title my investments to a limited partnership, can I also encumber the investments to add protection as you suggest with real estate and other assets?

Yes, and in some instances you should encumber investments titled to a limited partnership or LLC. Most frequently, we equity-strip real estate and other tangibles. But oftentimes, we encumber investments and other assets as well. One method would be to cross-collateralize real estate loans by pledging your investments (stock, bonds, etc.) as additional collateral. You can also equity-strip publicly-traded shares by borrowing on margin (up to 50 percent of share value). One danger from pledging your investment assets to secure real estate or business loans is that the lender has direct recourse to your investments should you default on your loan. For that reason, you want to collateralize these loans only to 'cooperative' lenders. Or you can borrow directly against your investments and safeguard the loan proceeds internationally. We have many ways to debt-shield liquid investments or any other asset.

Is life insurance and/or annuities creditor protected?

Some states fully protect the cash value and death benefits from life insurance and annuities, provided you buy them *before* you incur the liability. A common protective strategy is to convert exposed investments into exempt or protected insurance or annuity products. We see many variations on this theme, and some are quite complex. For example, international private placement variable universal life insurance policies (IPPVULIs) are popular planning tools. Or you can structure private annuity contracts to convert exposed assets into less exposed future or deferred income streams which would be less valuable to creditors. Similarly, IRS qualified international private placement deferred variable annuity contracts give you tax deferral and protection, as well as greater investment flexibility. Other planning opportunities exist with insurance-related products. And they are worth considering if these products meet your financial objectives beyond lawsuit-proofing. But you must ask your financial advisors about these insurance/annuity based strategies to avoid unintended tax or other planning pitfalls. Also consider whether these products are right for you both from an investment and tax viewpoint.

Are international annuities more protected?

Yes – if you buy them from insurers in the right jurisdiction. Some international annuities are self-protected. For example, you cannot lose to creditors a Swiss annuity if it has a proper one year advance beneficiary designation to a spouse or children revocably, or irrevocably, or third parties irrevocably. A court cannot compel you as the policyholder to liquidate the Swiss annuity and repatriate the funds. As the policyholder, you're powerless to do so. The Swiss annuity thus enjoys built-in protection against all creditors and judgments – including divorce. This broad protection is especially appealing when other asset plans offer more limited protection. But a little-known secret is that other international annuities are even more protective. While Swiss annuities have long symbolized quality and protection, Isle of Man and Lichtenstein insurers are as highly-rated as Swiss insurers and provide more protection. You should investigate the wide range of international investments. Your safest investment may be an international annuity, which may be considered for your investment portfolio. Unfortunately, too few Americans know about their financial and legal benefits. Of course, you would own your annuity or international portfolio through an international asset protection structure – such as an international asset protection trust – to add to the annuity's protection. The trust or international LLC would own the annuity and be its irrevocable beneficiary. You would name the trust's beneficiaries and retain the right to re-designate beneficiaries without losing protection. As an example, an Isle of Man annuity owned by an international trust and/or international LLC gives you exceptionally strong wealth

118

protection. Many of our clients have 'protected international portfolios'. The product is not necessarily an annuity, but an investment portfolio that meets our clients' investment needs and is issued from a rated underwriter in a jurisdiction that protects these investments from creditor seizure.

How can layering maximize my investment protection?

We often 'layer' the protection of our clients' investments. For example, we may title the investments to a limited partnership. The limited partnership is then owned by an IAPT as the limited partner. The IAPT, in turn, invests these funds through a Nevis or Cook Island LLC as its subsidiary. Finally, the LLC may buy an international annuity or self-protected investment portfolio. This provides four layers of protection and, of course, *very* well-insulated funds. We can design hundreds of different layering possibilities. But how far we go to protect one's investments depends on how much protection they need.

From our conversation it appears that you mostly recommend limited partnerships and/or international entities as the way to lawsuit-proof investments, but what about other possible options?

As with any type asset, there are multiple protective options. For instance, a few states with tenancy-by-the-entirety laws protect spousal co-owned investments from creditor claims against one spouse. Florida is one such state. But it's important that every asset (bank accounts, portfolio, etc.) be properly titled to gain this protection. Some spouses prefer to title their investments to the less vulnerable spouse. We think that this is poor planning for the same reason that titling the home and other real estate to one spouse is less than optimum. It creates estate planning difficulties and does not always safeguard the assets titled to that one spouse. A few of our clients have transferred their assets to irrevocable domestic trusts. This has the decided disadvantage of lost control over the transferred asset. It can also trigger gift taxes and other unwanted consequences. But for some people the irrevocable trust can provide counter-balancing estate planning, tax planning or charitable gifting benefits. We can talk more about trusts when we discuss ways to shelter one's estate. As with any asset – you need *your* one best strategy.

7

Protecting

Retirement Accounts

For many people retirement accounts are their major asset. How can these accounts be protected?

At one time much of America's net worth was in retirement accounts – particularly ERISA plans. But to answer your question, we plan in context to a client's state laws because the extent to which their plans are lawsuit-proof depends largely upon state law.

But we can generally discuss the protection for retirement accounts. First, we must divide retirement plans into: 1) ERISA-qualified plans, and 2) non-qualified retirement plans. Non-qualified plans include Individual Retirement Accounts (IRAs), Roth IRAs and SEP IRAs. *ERISA*-qualified plans are retirement accounts under the Employee Retirement Income Security Act of 1974 (ERISA). ERISA pension or profit sharing plans are spendthrift trusts. Their beneficiary cannot gift, anticipate or encumber the plan's principal or income. This spendthrift provision immunizes the plan from creditor claims. Qualified retirement plans include profit sharing plans (defined contribution plans), pension plans (defined benefit plans) and 401K and 403B plans (plans where the employee makes voluntary contributions). But not every ERISA pension plan is lawsuit-proof. To be protected, the company owners *and* at least one non-related employee must be covered under the plan. Technical deficiencies and non-compliance issues may also disqualify 401K and similar plans

121

from ERISA protection. That's why it's important to have your asset protection lawyer or plan administrator review your pension plan. You can't assume that it is protected.

IRAs, Roths and SEP-IRAs are not ERISA protected. Their protection against creditors depends upon state law. As with the state homestead, insurance, wage, and other exemptions, the state laws vary. Some states fully protect non-qualified retirement accounts, but most states partially protect non-qualified plans, usually for a statutory amount (i.e., $50,000), or for such amounts the court considers necessary to support the debtor's retirement. Other limitations or restrictions may apply under your state statutes. Several states protect accounts held in trust, but not distributions made to the beneficiary. So whether *your* retirement plan is lawsuit-proof depends upon: 1) whether your plan is qualified under the Employee Retirement Income Security Act (ERISA); 2) whether your state law exempts non-ERISA plans (i.e. IRAs), and for how much; 3) whether your plan is a pension or welfare benefit plan; 4) whether it's in payment mode or still in trust; 5) what creditor is claiming the retirement account; and 6) whether you are in bankruptcy. Fortunately, if your state doesn't adequately protect non-ERISA retirement accounts, you have other lawsuit-proofing options.

Does bankruptcy change my retirement plan's protection?

Recent bankruptcy law changes have expanded the lawsuit protection for IRAs. The new rules protect IRA rollovers from tax-qualified plans, regardless of where the IRA owner resides. The new bankruptcy law further exempts from creditor claims IRAs up to one million dollars, as well as IRAs and IRA earnings for larger amounts as may be determined by the bankruptcy court as necessary for the debtor's support. Simple retirement accounts, a simplified employee pension (SEPs) and 'rollovers' to the IRA from a qualified plan or another IRA are disregarded under this million dollar limit. Stated differently, the part of your IRA attributable to assets 'rolled over' from a tax-qualified plan and earnings on those rolled over assets – typically all or a large portion of the IRA assets – *are* protected, even if it exceeds one million dollars.

Isn't a pension safer in a 401K plan rather than a rollover IRA if my
state only shields IRAs, say up to $50,000?

From a protection viewpoint, that's true. But it's not necessarily true from an investment viewpoint. If you question the safety of your IRA under your state law, then it's safer not to rollover your pension into a self-directed IRA. Rolling over your ERISA-qualified funds to a self-directed IRA that your state doesn't fully protect reduces or eliminates your protection. Of course, you can't always keep retirement accounts in an employer's 401K plan. Or you may want to self-direct your IRA investments. The 'rollover' decision should primarily be an investment issue, but do consider asset protection. Also remember that the million-dollar exemption for IRAs doesn't include rollovers. And the exemption applies only in bankruptcy. If you're not in bankruptcy, and your state doesn't fully protect your IRA, you can lose the unprotected portion of your IRA – including rollovers.

For lawsuit protection, can I roll back my IRA into a 401K?

It can sometimes be wise to roll back your IRA into a qualified plan. And you can do this if your IRA was originally a rollover from an ERISA-qualified plan. Or you can set up your own qualified plan. Alternately, you can set up a tax compliant zero percent ERISA-qualified *and* creditor proof money purchase plan. Similarly, if your pension plan isn't creditor protected (i.e. a single-member plan), then you can add beneficiaries to make it creditor proof.

Are Roth IRAs as well-protected as IRAs?

SEP-IRAs and Roth IRAs don't necessarily have the same state statutory protection as do regular IRAs. Here's why. The newer Roth plans came about after the states enacted legislation to protect regular IRAs. So under some state laws, Roths or SEPs are not specifically referred to in the state exemption statutes. But most states have since amended their laws to also protect Roths and SEPs. If you have a Roth or SEP IRA, this is one question to investigate. Don't simply assume it's shielded to the extent IRAs are sheltered.

For added protection can I title my IRA to a limited liability company?

You can invest unprotected IRAs, SEP-IRAs or deferred compensation plan funds into a domestic *single*-member limited liability company (LLC). This gives your retirement funds 'charging order protection.' However, your plan custodian must agree to this. However, the IRA transfer can be recoverable from the LLC by a *present* creditor as a fraudulent transfer so you shouldn't rely on this strategy if you have an *existing* creditor. However, a single-member domestic LLC can somewhat protect your retirement funds against *future* creditors.

Would an international LLC better protect my IRA than a domestic LLC?

Yes. For stronger protection you should invest your retirement funds into an international LLC. Your IRA will be better protected than if you invest in a domestic LLC. Here's how the international LLC strategy works: Your retirement plan (IRA) would set up an international LLC. Your IRA custodian would then invest your IRA funds into the international LLC in exchange for the entire LLC membership. Then *no* retirement funds are within the U.S., subject to creditor claims. Your retirement account instead owns only the full membership interest in the international LLC. This membership interest is subject only to the charging order remedy. However, you can be the investment advisor and even a co-signatory on the international LLC account, *until* you have a judgment creditor. You can also safely reinvest your international LLC's funds in U.S. investments. The U.S. courts cannot compel you or your custodian to turn over the IRA funds because the international LLC owns the funds, and an international manager controls the LLC. If you have a substantial IRA that is unprotected by your state, then strongly consider this international LLC strategy.

However, even with the international LLC-IRA you must comply with all IRA rules because the IRA remains in full effect. All that has happened is that the IRA's sole asset now consists of the ownership of an international LLC, which in turn, invests the LLC funds. But the funds itself are owned by the international LLC managed by an international manager. Of course, we have excellent custodians who can oversee this arrangement. And as with the U.S.-based LLC, you can take your withdrawals from your international LLC-IRA. You'll experience no difference other than your IRA will be fully protected against virtually all claims.

If IRAs are not as fully protected in my state as annuities are, should my IRA buy an annuity?

Many states fully exempt annuities against lawsuits but don't similarly protect IRAs. If that's your state law, then you might consider investing your IRA in annuities. You wouldn't ordinarily buy annuities for your IRA because you only duplicate the tax deferral advantage. However, buying a self-protected annuity for an IRA can make sense when protection is your primary goal. This is one exception to the general rule not to invest an IRA in a tax deferred investment. But if you do foresee a lawsuit; it's an option. Similarly, you can annuitize your retirement plan which may be advantageous if your state better protects annuities. But is this a sound investment decision? That's why the reader must discuss this with their financial *and* asset protection advisors.

When is bankruptcy a good option to protect my retirement account?

As we say, bankruptcy may be the right option when you have a large and exposed retirement account and a sizeable potential debt.

When is it sensible to liquidate my IRA rather than lose it to a creditor?

If your IRA can be imminently seized and bankruptcy isn't a good alternative, your most practical solution may be to terminate your IRA, and pay the tax and early withdrawal penalty. You can then protect the proceeds as you'd shelter cash or other liquid investments. Dissolution is certainly the most economical option for the small

IRA which can't cost-justify more complex or costly protection. And you might avoid the early withdrawal penalty if you use the withdrawal or IRA borrowing exception rules to remove the money from your retirement account.

Do people with exposed IRAs ever liquidate their exposed IRAs and invest the proceeds in fully homestead protected homes – such as in Texas and Florida?

For some people who do have sizeable claims and equally sizeable unprotected retirement accounts, an alternative may be to relocate and invest the proceeds in a homestead. When you're at risk of losing your large retirement account you essentially must choose between three options: 1) Invest the IRA in an international LLC; 2) file bankruptcy; or 3) shift the retirement account proceeds into other exempt assets. This may be a homestead or possibly insurance products. Which is the best option? As with any plan, that depends on the client and the particulars of his case.

How should I proceed to better protect my IRA and Keogh plans?

To begin, add spendthrift provisions to your plan. Not every plan has this. Secondly, don't be the plan's sole trustee. Add another trustee. It can be your spouse. Thirdly, don't borrow money from your retirement account. If you owe money to your plan, repay it. Finally, don't control your retirement account. Maintain an 'arms-length' relationship with your plan. Each of these steps will help creditor proof a plan, but even when you take each of these steps, your plan may not be conclusively protected.

If my state fully protects IRAs, can I invest more than the allowed annual amount into my IRA to protect the surplus cash?

That can sometimes be a smart way to lawsuit-proof your extra cash – assuming your retirement plan is fully creditor protected. There are limits as to how much you can put into your retirement plan annually on a tax-deferred basis, but you can invest unlimited *after-tax* dollars into a lawsuit-proof retirement plan. Once you reach the permitted tax-deferred limit, you would pay the tax on your excess contributions. But these surplus funds would still be protected by your plan. You're never too young to 'grow' your retirement account. But do be careful. 'Accelerating' contributions into an IRA has its limitations. Some states will not creditor protect excess funds invested in retirement accounts shortly before bankruptcy or creditor seizure.

Can I use a trust to ensure that my spouse and children receive my retirement account free from creditor claims?

Yes, but you must use a 'retirement account trust' or an irrevocable trust with specific beneficiaries. A qualified plan funds are protected within your lifetime. Thereafter the trust shelters the funds from your own and your beneficiaries' creditors. You may designate your children or any other party as the residual beneficiaries.

Are deferred compensation plans creditor proof?

Yes. And you can defer a significant portion of your compensation under a non-qualified retirement or deferred compensation plan. Deferred compensation plans are safe from your own creditors, but not the claims of your employer's creditors. So consider this before you invest in a deferred compensation plan. There are, however, methods for an employer to lawsuit-proof a deferred compensation plan. For instance, the employer can hold the deferred compensation funds in an international 'rabbi' trust. This trust would then invest in one or more 'charging order only entities,' such as an international LLC to insulate the funds from the employer's creditors.

Are 412(i) plans also creditor protected?

A 412(i) or employer sponsored, tax qualified plan, is either a defined contribution or defined benefit plan. 412(i) plans are funded with life insurance and annuity contracts. There's no limit on contributions to a 412(i) plan, provided it covers the minimum insurance annuity premiums. One advantage of the 412(i) plan: you can make significantly larger annual contributions than under other retirement plans. This, of course, adds protection. Still, a 412(i) plan isn't for everyone. However, we do recommend it for older self-employed or professionals who earn above $250,000 a year; have few employees; and want significant tax, as well as lawsuit protection benefits.

You mentioned encumbering or equity-stripping other assets as a protective strategy. Can you also encumber retirement accounts?

You cannot normally encumber ERISA-qualified plans because of the spendthrift provisions, but then again there would be no need to protect ERISA-qualified plans. It is different with non-ERISA plans. To the extent there is exposure for the plan, the retirement account holder's interest can be encumbered. Therefore, encumbering an unprotected retirement account is a worthwhile strategy in some instances. In a few instances, we combined the international LLC-IRA strategy with encumbering the investments in the LLC. It builds a strong defense.

Of the various protective strategies that you mentioned for non-ERISA retirement accounts, which do you most generally use?

Our own firm generally prefers the international LLC strategy. This protects the IRA from any creditor. We also recommend that the international LLC invest the IRA proceeds with a creditor protected investment portfolio from a jurisdiction that shelters these accounts. We have other strategies that can protect distributions from the IRA, such as distributions to domestic LLCs and limited partnerships. What is important with any strategy is that it be reviewed by a retirement account specialist to ascertain that the plan remains fully tax-compliant.

What do you see as the greatest danger to retirement accounts?

The greatest danger is taxes – not creditors. Few people realize that they can lose upwards of 80 percent of their retirement accounts to a series of federal and state taxes that can be imposed on these accounts. Whenever we have a client with a large retirement account, we refer them to financial planners – particularly those knowledgeable about retirement planning. There are a number of ways to lessen the tax bite. Our urging our clients to get that advice is oftentimes our most important contribution to preserving their retirement funds.

8

Protecting Your
Estate or Inheritance

How does estate planning fit in with asset protection planning?

The two objectives are closely connected. You can work a lifetime to accumulate your wealth and lose it all to your creditors after you die. Or you can lose it to your children's creditors or ex-spouses. Children do lose their parents' hard-earned money. Without careful planning you can also lose a fortune in estate taxes. So you must also think about how you can best protect your assets *after* you pass on. We want our clients to look ahead. How can they shield their wealth from creditors and wasteful heirs after they're gone? On the other hand, you may be a beneficiary of a large inheritance. You must then ask yourself similar questions. How should you safeguard your inheritance against your financial problems? What would happen to your inheritance if you divorce? How can you protect your inheritance once you're ready to pass it on to *your* heirs? These matters take careful thought.

Of course, how you protect your assets during your lifetime takes one set of strategies. How you should lawsuit-proof and safeguard your wealth after you die demands other strategies. Many large estates have been squandered by heirs, or ravaged by litigation only because the decedents didn't give enough forethought to the disposition of their estate. Estate planning, of course, is itself a highly-complex specialty. And as with lawsuit protection planning, you have countless planning options. And as with asset protection, you must customize your estate plan to your specific needs. That's why we integrate estate planning with our asset protection plans.

What happens to my assets if I don't plan my estate?

The first step to protecting any estate is to have a current estate plan. To die without a will only invites legal problems. Everyone needs at least a last will. Most people can probably also benefit from a living trust to pass their estate to their intended beneficiaries without probate. Without a will or trust your assets will pass by intestacy under your state laws, and this may not be in the manner you wish. Without a will you also lose the opportunity to name your executor or guardian for your minor children. You also lose the opportunity to lower your estate taxes if you don't plan your estate. For those reasons you should review your will and/or living trust annually, upon marriage, divorce, birth of a child, relocation, the death of your spouse, whenever your financial situation changes or wish to change how you want to leave your assets.

Estate plans, like asset protection plans, can change frequently. And an outdated estate plan can cause more serious legal problems than dying intestate. Just writing your last will usually isn't enough either. A comprehensive plan will also include a durable power of attorney – one for healthcare and another for financial/legal affairs – to appoint someone to represent you if you become incapacitated. Finally, a living will can express when you want your life artificially prolonged. Having a good estate planner is vital, especially if you have a large or complex estate.

How can creditors be prevented from claiming an estate?

While most people fully pay their final debts from their estate, some folks do have more debts than assets when they die. Other decedents may have pending lawsuits against them, or are sued *after* they die. Your goal then is to arrange your affairs so that your assets will pass to your heirs free of lawsuit or creditor claims. There are ways to accomplish this. One option is to title your property jointly or as tenancy-by-the-entirety. In most states, jointly owned property passes to the surviving joint owner free of creditor claims against the deceased owner, though there are exceptions. Titling assets jointly with right of survivorship (JTWROS), or as husband and wife as tenants-by-the-entirety is only one option when you want your interest in property to pass creditor free upon your death to your surviving co-owner. Another option is to bequeath your property through an irrevocable trust that you fund during your lifetime and *before* you have creditors, as later transfers to the trust may be recoverable by the creditor as a fraudulent transfer. Your trust, of course, must also be protectively structured. Still another option is to make lifetime gifts to deplete your estate – provided these gifts aren't fraudulent transfers. Another option is to invest in fixed annuities or other investments that transform your wealth into an exempt income stream for yourself or your heirs. Its death benefit – or future payments – would pass debt-free to your survivors and sidestep creditor claims.

Can a living trust lawsuit-proof my assets?

No. The living trust is a good way to avoid the cost and delay of probate and it can also avoid the problems of joint ownership. However, living trusts are usually *revocable,* and therefore they give you, as the grantor, *no asset protection* because they are revocable. If you can revoke your trust, your creditors can 'step into your shoes' and also unwind the trust. If you have a living trust or any other revocable trust your creditors *can* claim its assets. Moreover, living trusts can cause you to *lose* your lawsuit protection in those few states that don't extend their homestead protection to homes that are titled to a living trust. Similarly, assets that are protectively owned as tenants-by-the-entirety lose this form of protection when those same assets are titled to a living trust.

The most common trust is the living trust, which is also known as the Family Trust, Loving Trust, or Revocable Inter Vivos Trust. As mentioned previously, the living trust's primary goal is to avoid probate of the grantor's assets when he or she dies, as well as provide for a means of managing the grantor's assets if the grantor becomes incapacitated. Avoiding the time and hassle of the court supervised process of distributing a deceased person's (decedent's) assets to their heirs may sound desirable, but are living trusts for everyone? The answer depends on the decedent's state of residence and the size of their estate. Some states, such as California, Delaware, Florida, and New York, have a relatively long and expensive probate process. However, other states, such as North Carolina, have a streamlined process. A small, simple estate in a state such as North Carolina may be inexpensively settled in as little as two to four weeks. However, probate of a more complex, large estate in a state such as California could drag out for a couple years, and legal and other costs could reach into the hundreds of thousands of dollars. Perhaps, one drawback of probate that's universal to all states is the fact that anyone who wants to may access the probate records (including a list of estate assets) during probate.

If an individual has had multiple marriages (especially if there are different children from different marriages), an estate over $500,000 in value, property located in multiple states, or a desire for privacy, then a living trust is probably a good idea.

As mentioned previously, living trusts are created during the grantor's lifetime, and the trust may be amended or revoked by the grantor anytime before he dies. The grantor thus retains complete control over trust assets during his lifetime, as well as the ability to receive as much income from the trust as he wishes. Oftentimes the grantor is the trust's trustee.

Because the grantor retains complete control over the trust assets, any gifts made to the trust are gift tax-free. However, there is a downside to retaining such control over a trust. First, any assets held in a living trust are included in the grantor's estate for the purposes of calculating the estate tax liability even though the assets are not included in the estate for probate purposes. Furthermore, living trusts provide very little asset protection, as it is standard procedure for a judge to order the grantor to revoke the trust so that all assets revert back to his ownership, thus becoming subject to creditor attachment. Remember: a creditor of a grantor can control or access trust assets to the same extent the grantor can.

133

Upon the grantor's death the trust becomes irrevocable, and if the grantor was the trustee then a new trustee is appointed in accordance with the trust. Usually a living trust includes a list of successor trustees for this very occasion. Upon the grantor's death, trust assets are normally distributed to heirs according to the provisions of the trust. However, this is not always the case. Some assets may be held in trust if the beneficiaries are still minors. Perhaps the assets are not distributed until the heirs are even older, or perhaps certain beneficiaries only receive income from the trust while it remains in force. Because trusts can be drafted in any manner to meet the grantor's needs, there will usually be some variation between trusts, even if they are the same type of trust. This flexibility is what gives trusts much of their power. If an heir is mentally challenged or otherwise disabled, for example, the trust could make sure that the heir's needs are met even after the grantor dies. Some living trusts contain provisions that will cause the creation of other trusts, or sub-trusts, upon some triggering event – usually the grantor's death. Credit shelter trusts are often created in such a manner.

Do certain assets, other than those titled to living trusts, also avoid probate?

Some assets do avoid probate even without the use of a living trust. These assets include:

- Property held as tenants-by-the-entirety (TBE) or as joint tenants with right of survivorship (JTWROS). Full ownership under these arrangements automatically pass to the surviving owner.
- Payable-on-death (POD) bank accounts are available in several, but not all states. Upon the owner's death, the proceeds go directly to the named beneficiary and bypass probate. The beneficiary may not access the funds before the owner's death; neither need he be aware of the account prior to the owner's death. These accounts are also known as *Totten Trusts*.

- Transfer-on-death (TOD) securities are also available in several states. Securities are transferred on death if these securities are registered appropriately, and the beneficiary provides a certified death certificate and a signature guarantee.

- Life insurance proceeds with a named beneficiary. However probate is not bypassed if the beneficiary is the estate.

- Retirement plans with a named beneficiary, unless the beneficiary is the estate.

These assets may or may not be creditor protected in a particular state, and in the event of litigation further steps may be necessary to shelter them. Also, it is often wise to designate a trust to be the beneficiary. This prevents waste of the asset in the event the monies are left outright to a spendthrift beneficiary.

Does this mean that one shouldn't use a living trust for estate planning?

No. They probably should use a living trust in their asset protection plan. The living trust can own FLPs, LLC memberships or other entities that do protect assets. The idea is to use corporations, trusts, FLPs, LLCs and other legal entities to protect your assets, such as real estate, stocks, bank accounts, and so forth. However, you or your family wouldn't personally own these entities. Your revocable living trust would own these entities so you can avoid probate on these entities when you die. You then get the best of both worlds. You have a protective entity to shield your assets during your lifetime, and the living trust will possibly save your family estate taxes and probate fees when you die.

Obviously, there are many different trusts. How does one know which trusts fit their circumstances?

Unfortunately, we couldn't possibly discuss all the different trusts in this interview. The most common use of trusts is for estate planning. Since asset protection planners know that asset protection works best when coupled with other legitimate purposes, using a trust to achieve both asset protection and estate planning results in a more formidable overall barrier against creditor threats, while efficiently meeting multiple objectives with a single strategy. It is not our objective to exhaustively review all estate planning trusts and how they will be treated in every situation, as doing so could fill a separate book in and of itself. But we can identify the major trust strategies available and what benefits and possible drawbacks each one generally provides. A competent estate planner should then be contacted in order to make a final determination as to a strategy's viability for an individual's particular circumstances.

Which trusts shelter assets from creditors?

As you now know, a revocable trust cannot give you asset protection. For creditor protection, you need an irrevocable trust. But the obvious disadvantage with an irrevocable trust is that you can't revoke the trust and reclaim your assets. You essentially lose control over the trust assets. Irrevocable trusts protect assets for the same reason that revocable trusts cannot. Your creditors can unwind the revocable living trust, but not the irrevocable trust. Therefore, irrevocable trust assets are generally safer from creditors and lawsuits. However, the irrevocable trust carries this heavy price of lost control over your assets. Most people consider that loss in control too steep of a price for protection. But you might use an irrevocable trust when you'd inevitably gift the assets to the beneficiaries anyway and you don't foresee needing the assets for yourself. Your 'price' then is not particularly heavy. You don't personally need the assets, and the trust accomplishes what you want – to distribute the assets to your beneficiaries (usually your children) at some future time. But keep four cautions in mind: 1) you can't reserve any power to revoke, rescind or amend the trust, or retain any direct or indirect rights to reclaim property transferred to the trust. In sum, there can be 'no strings attached'; 2) you can't dictate how the trust property will be managed or invested; 3) you can't be the trustee, nor can you appoint your spouse, relative or close personal friend to be the trustee. Your trustee must be arms-length. 4) In most states you cannot be the beneficiary as this creates a self-settled trust.

Alaska and Delaware promote domestic asset protection trusts (DAPTs). Are they more protective than others?

Alaska, Delaware and a few other domestic asset protection trust (DAPT) jurisdictions encourage the formation of trusts in their states. These DAPT jurisdictions promise added estate planning and asset protection benefits. It is a good idea to explore the estate tax advantages of these DAPTs – particularly if their state has an inheritance tax. DAPTs are primarily promoted as alternatives to the international trust. Undoubtedly, some Americans are more comfortable with a U.S.-based trust rather than an international trust. This appears to be the DAPT's chief selling point. Several other states also have good DAPT laws. For instance, Rhode Island, Colorado and Nevada have excellent DAPT laws. But in most respects, the DAPT laws of Delaware, Rhode Island, Nevada and Alaska closely compare.

DAPTs offer certain estate planning advantages but DAPTs aren't, in our opinion, always sufficiently protective. For example, DAPTs won't necessarily protect you against *present* creditors. And DAPTs are far less protective than international trusts because an international trustee won't enforce U.S. judgments or court orders. On the other hand, state trustees *must* constitutionally recognize and enforce judgments and court orders from other states. For example, if an asset that you transfer to a DAPT is ruled a fraudulent transfer in your state, the trust assets are likely recoverable by a creditor who challenges the transfer in the trust state. If you do set up a domestic asset protection trust, then, at the very least, include within the trust a 'migration' clause, which allows you to relocate the DAPT to an international jurisdiction if there's a creditor challenge. DAPTs also have restrictions – such as residency requirements. Your money, the trustee, the settlor (or all three) must usually be situated within that DAPT state.

The major advantage of the DAPT is that they can be self-settled; that is the grantor can also be a beneficiary. This arrangement, in these DAPT states only, does not detract from the trust's protection as it would in all other states. On the downside, many asset protection planners believe that the DAPT would still be vulnerable to a creditor who can claim a fraudulent transfer. Since it is a relatively new entity, we will have to wait and see how protective the DAPT is in practice. In the meantime, we continue to prefer the international trust.

Here's a question that you are probably frequently asked. How can one protect their children from losing their inheritance?

This is an important and common question. You can spend your lifetime scrimping, saving, and sheltering your wealth, and leave your fortune to your kids who promptly spend or lose it. So you must also safeguard your beneficiary's inheritance. For this you'll need a spendthrift trust. The spendthrift trust will protect your beneficiary's interest in the trust from his or her judgment creditors and ex-spouses, since there is an *anti-alienation* or *spendthrift* clause in the trust to protect the trust assets from a beneficiary's creditors. The anti-alienation provision prohibits the trustee from distributing trust assets to anyone other than the beneficiary. This would include the beneficiary's creditors. The spendthrift and anti-alienation provisions expressly preclude anyone whose interest is adverse to the beneficiary (a creditor, ex-spouse, etc.) from claiming the beneficiary's share of the trust principal or income. However, these provisions don't always give a beneficiary absolute protection. There are limitations. For example, several states don't recognize or enforce spendthrift provisions. Nor do spendthrift provisions always fully protect a beneficiary. Nor does it shelter income distributions once paid to the beneficiary.

Equally important, in our view, is to give the trustee the discretion to withhold distributions to the beneficiary. For example, if your trust provides a beneficiary trust distribution at age 25, will those distributions be safe if the beneficiary has a judgment creditor or pending divorce when the beneficiary reaches 25? A discretionary provision allows the trustee to withhold income and principal distributions that would otherwise be paid to the beneficiary if the trustee believes the funds would be lost to the beneficiary's creditors. A discretionary clause also prevents a beneficiary from wasting trust assets; an especially important consideration when your children are the beneficiaries and you want your trustee to control distributions

138

to your children. If your child isn't a spendthrift, is your child's spouse? You see the point. You also want to preserve the trust principal for your child in the event your child dies or divorces and similarly want to protect gifts you place in trust for your grandchildren or great-grandchildren.

We also commonly add sprinkling provisions to trusts that are expected to last ten or more years and where each beneficiary's future income or tax situation is uncertain. This sprinkling provision lets the trustee modify trust distributions to determine what, and when, each beneficiary receives their distributions. But you – as the grantor – would set the criteria for the trustee's distributions and specify minimum income distributions when the beneficiary is your spouse or dependent.

Are there potential benefits to using an international trust for estate planning?

Definitely. One advantage is that it gives the settlor and the beneficiaries more formidable protection during their lifetime. Another advantage of the international trust is that they may save taxes for the grantor's heirs. A properly structured international trust will, upon the grantor's death, become an irrevocable trust not subject to U.S. taxation as long as it derives no U.S.-source income. Established in the correct jurisdiction, the trust may forever be free of U.S. income and estate taxes after the grantor's death; however, the beneficiaries are taxed on distributions from the trust when they receive them. If such a trust exists perpetually, for example, as a 'dynasty trust', these benefits may be substantial. Having such a purpose for an international trust is a unique non-asset protection benefit that no domestic trust can provide.

Despite the potential estate planning and other benefits an international trust may provide, one must be careful not to use an IAPT to save on income taxes. The Small Business Job Protection Act of 1996 restricted the tax benefits available to international trusts, by making it so that any transfer of assets by a U.S. person to an international trust would make that trust subject to the IRS's grantor tax rules. This means the trust's grantor must pay taxes on all trust income worldwide as if that income was actually received by the grantor himself. Finally, the international trust can be structured to accomplish what can be accomplished by any domestic trust, and, of course, the international trust would include testamentary provisions to distribute the trust assets upon the death of the settlor.

Do you frequently recommend children's trusts for minor children as a protective tool?

An irrevocable children's trust's (ICT) advantage is that it can reduce your income tax and give you some lawsuit protection. The children's trust assets cannot be claimed by your creditors, unless you fraudulently transfer your assets to the trust. Nor will these assets be included in your taxable estate. Moreover, the trust income is taxed at your children's lower tax rates. While the trust is in effect and until the beneficiary reaches 21, neither the grantor nor the child's creditors can claim the trust assets. But one disadvantage with the children's trust is that when your child turns 21, the child can claim the trust assets. The trust is also irrevocable; therefore you can't prevent your child from claiming the trust assets. For these reasons you must carefully consider whether your child or children can properly and responsibly handle trust assets at age 21. You no more want to lose trust assets to an irresponsible 21-year-old than to a lawsuit.

How can I make lifetime gifts to my children to reduce my taxable estate, retain control over the assets, and also gain creditor protection?

You'll lose control over your money during your lifetime if you make outright gifts to your kids. You understand the dangers. However, funding an irrevocable trust may not be your answer either, as you will lose control. A smarter solution may be to title your assets to a limited partnership with you and/or your spouse as its general partner. You would then annually transfer a percentage of the limited partnership interest to your children's irrevocable trust. This allows you to reduce your taxable estate each year as you continue to shift your wealth in the form of limited partnership interests to your children's trusts. Your assets will remain safe from *your* creditors because your assets are titled to a limited partnership. You will continue to control the assets because you are the general partner of the limited partnership. Your children's interest will be twice protected from legal and financial problems – once by the limited partnership and again by their spendthrift trust. When you die, your remaining partnership interest will have a discounted value for estate tax purposes. You can also then leave your remaining limited partnership interest, or any part thereof, to your children's' trust. We have hundreds of ways to combine trusts, FLPs, LLCs, corporations and other entities to achieve nearly any asset protection and estate planning objective and our estate planning attorneys are quite expert at this.

How can I protect the inheritances I leave to a spouse?

A frequent estate planning objective is to prevent a spouse from losing his or her inheritance. You may also want to insure that your spouse will eventually bequeath your assets to beneficiaries of your choice which are usually children from a former marriage. To accomplish this calls for a Q-Tip or Qualified Terminable Interest Property trust which gives your spouse lifetime income from the trust. But once your spouse dies or remarries, the trust principal passes to your children or whatever other beneficiaries that you designate.

Q-TIPs are common with subsequent marriages because they preserve the assets for the grantor's children rather than the spouse's children or family who would otherwise logically become the beneficiaries if the deceased spouse's estate were left outright to the surviving spouse. Q-TIPs can also be used for first spouses when the concern is that the surviving spouse may be sued or waste the assets. A Q-TIP is essentially a spendthrift trust to shelter the deceased spouse's assets from the surviving spouse's creditors or subsequent mates. One restriction is that income from the Q-TIP trust must be used solely to benefit the surviving spouse during the spouse's lifetime. That's vital if the trust is to qualify for the unlimited marital deduction. However Q-TIP trusts won't protect your assets from your creditors –

assuming you are the grantor – because Q-TIP is a *testamentary* trust. It's funded only upon your death, and the assets remain in your own name and vulnerable to your creditors during your lifetime. However, the Q-TIP trust can shelter your wealth from a spendthrift spouse, or spouse who has legal difficulties after you die.

Are gifts to charity through a charitable remainder trust creditor protected?

The Charitable Remainder Trust (CRT) allows you to gift your property to charity, protect it from your creditors, save taxes, receive a lifetime income, and still leave your heirs whatever amount you gifted to charity. As the trust grantor, you select a tax-exempt charitable organization as the beneficiary of the CRT. By funding the trust, you make a charitable donation and earn a tax deduction. As the lifetime income beneficiary, the trust will pay you an annual income. Thus, you get an immediate tax deduction and a lifetime income stream.

If you donate assets to a CRT, you roughly get the same income, and can deduct the donation as a charitable contribution. The taxes saved through the deduction, can buy life insurance to give your heirs about the same amount they would receive had you not funded the CRT. CRTs are especially sensible when you have appreciated assets and want a fixed income for your retirement. If you want to give to charity, the CRT can be an effective tax-saver, asset protector and income generator. There are also several variations on the CRT that you may consider with your estate planner.

How can I best accelerate my lifetime gifting to my children to reduce my taxable estate and also to have less money vulnerable to my prospective creditors?

Accelerated lifetime gifting can reduce your estate taxes and also protect those assets you don't need to support your lifestyle. Gifting may also shift your assets to a less liability-prone recipient and even save you income taxes if you transfer your income-producing assets to recipients in a lower tax bracket. The present annual gift tax exclusion of $14,000 annually per recipient is tax-free, provided your gift is immediately available to the recipient. For example, a couple with three children can gift to their children $84,000 annually, tax-free. To accelerate your gifts you can transfer property in exchange for an installment sale note (a SCIN) that would be payable annually. Each year you can forgive $14,000 per recipient without tax consequences. Ultimately, the note self-liquidates. This asset transfer would be a 'fair consideration' exchange (the note) and therefore not fraudulent against creditors. But to keep the note safe from creditors, one should title it to a family limited partnership. It's best to also gift those assets that are most vulnerable to creditors and retain exempt or otherwise protected assets.

How can beneficiaries prevent their creditors from seizing their future inheritance?

That's an excellent – and often overlooked – question. One option is to disclaim their inheritance. A beneficiary who disclaims their inheritance essentially passes the inheritance to the next generation. The disclaimer is a good strategy when you want your children to receive your inheritance rather than lose it to your creditors. A disclaimer is a complete, unqualified refusal to accept rights or property. You can disclaim both gifts and inheritances. Your alternate beneficiary may be your children, spouse or whoever else you designate to receive the gift. Your disclaimer must be in writing and you must not have already accepted any part of the property or any other ownership benefits. Your disclaimer also must be received by the transferor within nine months from when the transfer or document creating the interest (the bequeath or gift) is made.

***For asset protection, couldn't an inheritance also be directed to a
protective entity on behalf of a beneficiary?***

Certainly. And it's often wise to do so. A testator who wants to safely bequeath wealth
to a beneficiary should direct the inheritance to any entity that would insulate the
inheritance from the beneficiary's creditors. For example, the gift may be bequeathed
through: 1) a domestic testamentary trust with spendthrift, anti-alienation and
discretionary provisions; 2) an integrated estate planning trust internationally; or 3) a
limited partnership or LLC. In each instance, the beneficiary can enjoy the full
benefits of the gift or bequest as the beneficiary, partner or member of those entities.
A beneficiary of a large inheritance must look ahead to protect their *future* wealth and
suggest these possibilities to those from whom they anticipate gifts.

What is the role of limited partnerships in estate planning?

One role is that it offers important estate tax benefits. FLP interests are subject to a
discounted valuation by the IRS. An FLP that owns an asset is considered to have less
value than the sum of its underlying assets. First, the IRS applies a *lack of
marketability* discount, since your FLP interest is not readily marketable; its value is
reduced for tax purposes. There's little market for FLP interests when the other
partners are family members. If you own less than 50 percent of the FLP, the IRS
then also applies the *minority ownership* discount to your FLP interest because
there's little market for FLP interests which others control. The result is that the IRS
may value your FLP interest 15 to 40 percent below your percentage fair market value
share. This can translate into a significant estate tax savings if you have a larger
estate. That's one reason we use FLPs to own LLCs, corporations and other assets.
The FLP can layer your creditor protection and also decrease your estate taxes.

144

I imagine that integrated asset protection/estate planning can be quite complex – particularly for the high net worth individual?

We have only summarily discussed trusts that have been traditionally used for either asset protection or estate planning purposes. As with most fields, new strategies are constantly being developed (this is akin to new technologies being developed in the world of science). But there are state-of-the-art, recent, cutting edge trust developments in estate and asset protection planning. Few planners are aware of these trusts. Even fewer – only a few nationwide – actually know how to implement and use them for maximum benefit. Our website www.AssetProtectionAttorneys.com discusses some of these cutting edge trusts for estate planning. And this is an important point. High net worth individuals must work with knowledgeable advisors to stay abreast of the new opportunities to better protect their assets and simultaneously plan their estate.

9

Protecting
Your Business or
Professional Practice

Protecting one's personal assets can certainly involve many different strategies. Let's talk for a few moments about businesses and professional practices.

How important is defensive planning for the small or mid-sized business or professional practice?

While lawsuit proofing is necessary for every individual, it is no less important for small businesses and professional practices. They are more vulnerable to lawsuits and creditor problems than individuals and need their own brand of financial protection. Unfortunately, few business owners go through the advanced planning necessary to blockade lawsuits and other inevitable financial threats that can sink their business. Business start-ups are the products of entrepreneurs, and entrepreneurs are fueled by optimism. They journey into business happily envisioning only the upside, seldom the downside. Because they are success-oriented, they ignore the possibility of failure and overlook the most obvious precautions necessary to protect themselves and their business when trouble strikes. Experienced businesspeople are more realistic. They reduce risk. They defensively position their enterprise as well as their personal assets because they know their business will have battles and inevitable wars with creditors and litigants. The well-fortified business always has the best chance to survive.

What portion of your clientele are small businesses?

About one-third, maybe more. We have judgment-proofed nearly every size and type business from $50 million manufacturers to tiny home-based businesses. Of course, with most of our cases involving the judgment-proofing of the business, we simultaneously judgment-proof the owner's personal assets. The two go hand-in-hand.

What types of liabilities or claims do businesses normally encounter?

Every type claim you can imagine. They get sued for breach of contract, negligence, product liability, employment violations, anti-trust, SEC violations, unpaid bills, stockholder actions – you name it. It still amazes us that so many businesses have done absolutely nothing to shield their enterprise considering the many legal and financial problems that they do encounter.

What is the first defensive step to take when you go into business?

Choose the right form of business entity. You need an entity that will limit your personal exposure. Usually the corporation or limited liability company (LLC) will best protect your personal assets from the debts and liabilities of the business. Still, many people venture into business without corporate or LLC protection and operate their venture as proprietorships or general partnerships. That's foolish. Why do these people needlessly gamble their personal assets on the success of their enterprise? Since most small companies fail, this is a very poor gamble. Nevertheless, millions of small American businesses are still unincorporated.

Why is this? One answer is that small business owners are often unsophisticated about business and legal matters. They don't always appreciate the importance of a corporation or LLC for their personal protection. And their attorneys also may overlook the hazards of business and fail to incorporate them. We also see accountants who are often more concerned about the added paperwork from incorporating than liability protection. They too discourage incorporating. However, incorporating your business is your *best* insurance. Only a corporation, LLC or similar limited liability business organization limits your potential losses to your investment in your business. If you operate your business as a sole proprietorship or general partnership, you and your business are considered one and the same. But why allow business creditors to claim your personal assets? If you want to protect your personal assets, set up a corporation, LLC or another protective entity to operate your business or professional practice. That's Cardinal Rule #1.

But what about the smaller enterprise – for example, the home-based business; does it also need to incorporate?

Positively. The fallacy is that the small business – usually a home-based service business – is too small to worry much about liability issues. What their owners don't realize is that even the smallest transaction can trigger an enormous liability which can cause the unprotected proprietor to lose all his or her personal assets. That's why we insist that every one of our business clients operate their enterprise through a protective entity. There are no exceptions – no matter how safe or small the business may be.

Which are the most popular entities for small business owners?

Before the advent of the LLC; the corporation was the only practical entity for the small business owner. The choice was then between the S corporation and the C corporation. Now the LLC is the third option. Most small business owners, in the past, elected the S corporation over the C corporation because the S corporation is taxed as a proprietorship or partnership so the profits or losses would flow directly to its stockholders. Larger corporations normally select the C corporation because of its number and diversity of stockholders. This prevents the business from operating as an S corporation. The C corporation, of course, carries the burden of double taxation. The C corporation pays taxes on its earnings and the dividends are taxed again to the stockholders when received.

Is there any difference between the S and C corporations for liability protection?

None whatsoever. They both provide the same limited liability to its stockholders. Many people think that because the S corporation is taxed as a proprietorship or partnership, it has the unlimited liability characteristics of these entities. Of course, that's untrue. It is true that it is more problematic to protect S corporation shares because these shares cannot be owned by limited partnerships, trusts and most other protective entities. But as we talked about earlier when we spoke about investments, we have several options to shelter S corporation shares – and they ought to be protected.

Why is the limited liability company gaining popularity as a business entity?

A limited liability company combines the advantages of a corporation with those of a limited partnership, but there are several reasons why a limited liability company may be preferable to either of these entities. One advantage is that you can avoid double taxation with a limited liability company. Since the limited liability company is not a corporation, you can avoid corporate income tax if you so choose, because income from the limited liability company can be taxed personally to its members as it would be with a partnership. As a hybrid entity, the LLC features both the limited liability advantage of the corporation with the favorable single income taxation of the partnership. More importantly, a member's interest in the limited liability company gives his creditors only the charging order remedy which is the same as with the limited partnership (LP). Because the limited liability company compares protectively

149

to the limited partnership, it is an equally attractive vehicle to title and protect personal assets. Moreover, since neither the limited liability company's managers nor its members have personal liability for the debts or liabilities of the limited liability company, it is oftentimes ideal to hold liability-producing assets or to conduct a business. Overall, the limited liability company offers several significant benefits over the corporation and other traditional forms of business organizations. But there are also several disadvantages with the LLC: First, limited liability companies do not enjoy the corporate advantages of prior IRS rulings concerning the sale of worthless stock or stock sold at a loss. Secondly, LLC membership interests do not enjoy the same 'discounted valuations' for estate tax purposes as limited partnership interests. Thirdly, selling 50 percent or more of the ownership of the limited liability company in any twelve-month period ends any tax advantages the limited liability company may have had with the IRS. Fourth, limited liability companies cannot engage in tax-free reorganizations. And finally, owners of limited liability companies pay higher unemployment taxes on their own earnings than do corporate officers.

As you can see, there is no one perfect entity. You must consider a wide range of factors when you decide upon your best organizational choice. And this decision should involve both your accountant and your attorney.

Which entities are the best liability insulators for professionals?

Professionals also have organizational options. Most of our doctor, dentist, lawyer and accountant clients prefer professional corporations (PC) or professional associations (PA) which limits their liability in the same way a corporation or LLC personally protects the business owner. While the professional corporation protects the professional from the debts of their practice; the professional corporation won't personally protect the professional sued for his or her own malpractice. Still, these entities can insulate the professional from errors by other employees, as well as from other corporate liabilities. Moreover, the professional corporation's assets cannot be directly claimed by the professional's personal creditors. Nor can the professional's personal creditors readily seize the professional's stock ownership in the professional

150

corporation since the ownership of these entities, by regulation, usually must be owned by professionals from that profession.

Another option is the limited liability partnership (LLP). They are similar to the LLC, but are, by state law, only for specified professionals. The LLP is an excellent option for professionals who want to manage their practice while insulating their personal assets from partnership liabilities. The professional's personal assets are protected when conducting their practice through a limited liability partnership. In contrast, the general partnership is the professional's most dangerous form of organization because each partner has unlimited personal liability for every partnership debt. Professionals in a general partnership should instead organize their own professional corporation. Their respective corporations can then become partners in a general partnership. Though this arrangement is more cumbersome than forming one limited liability partnership, it may provide certain tax, regulatory or organizational advantages. The point is that no professional today can rely solely upon malpractice insurance for protection. Professionals incur too many other liabilities in their practice. They need the same sound organizational protection as do business owners.

Many people claim that there are advantages to incorporating in Nevada. Is that true?

We are frequently asked this question. Corporations are creations of state law and state laws differ. It can sometimes be advantageous to incorporate in a particular state. If your corporation operates an active business in only one state, then it's probably best to incorporate in that state, since out-of-state corporations must register as an international corporation in the home state where it will do business. But if you have flexibility as to where to incorporate, Nevada is a good choice. So is Delaware. Many of America's largest corporations incorporate in Delaware, with its exceptionally debtor-friendly laws. Delaware also offers certain tax advantages for larger corporations. However, the smaller business may find Nevada more advantageous; (though Wyoming's corporate laws follow Nevada's). Nevada is state tax-free. Most importantly, Nevada's corporate officers and directors have broader liability protection. For example, Nevada corporations limit the personal liability of officers and directors for breach of fiduciary duty (other than improper dividend payments). Nevada imposes a short statute of limitations for creditors to sue. Nevada also allows broader indemnities for officers or even stockholders who incur liability on behalf of the corporation. For instance, corporate directors can take a security interest or lien on corporate assets to guarantee their indemnifications. This can be quite useful for asset protection. Other states invalidate these self-serving legal arrangements. Nevada also better protects the corporate shares. It limits a stockholder's creditor to a charging order, in the same way an LLC does. That feature is unique to Nevada. But no state is perfect. For instance, Nevada corporations have double the IRS audit rate. And contrary to myth, you really can't issue bearer shares with Nevada corporations to disguise your ownership. So the choice of jurisdiction as to where to incorporate is a mixed bag. It involves a number of considerations that must be decided by both your attorney and accountant.

For lawsuit protection should I privatize my ownership in the corporation?

Shareholders do often attempt to camouflage their ownership interest. Yet more diligent creditors can usually identify the corporate shareholders by examining the corporate books, tax returns, licensing applications, public records and so forth. But you can somewhat privatize your ownership in a corporation. For instance, you may have your corporation owned by another domestic corporation, international corporation, LLC or trust from an international financial center that has secrecy laws. These entities can be the parent or holding company. But your lawyer must guide you on these strategies. You don't want to commit perjury, incur tax problems or violate IRS reporting rules concerning international entities by camouflaging your ownership. And for less visibility and connection to your corporation, use a 'nominee' corporate officer and director. The best strategy, of course, is to *protect* your stock ownership, not *conceal* it.

How can corporate creditors be discouraged from trying to pierce the corporate veil to sue its officers or owners personally?

Corporate creditors oftentimes do personally sue business owners to collect on corporate debts. To do so, corporate creditors attempt to 'pierce the corporate veil' to recover from their owners' personal assets, claiming their owners are only *alter-egos* of their corporation. And they can succeed if you ignore the basic corporate formalities. So it's important to operate your corporation, or any other legal entity, as an independent entity – one that is distinct from you personally or any other entity. For example, you should never commingle assets. You must document every financial transaction between yourself and your company, as well as related corporations. And sign your corporate documents as a corporate agent, add your corporate name and title aside your signature on all documents, and keep good corporate records. Nor should you ever *voluntarily* dissolve your corporation or you'll then lose your corporate protection as your corporation's debts will become your personal obligations. Finally, you want to observe all corporate formalities. For instance, does your corporation have its own business address? Telephone number? Does your corporation pay its own expenses? Does it have the necessary business licenses? Bank accounts? Each point establishes that your corporation or LLC is a legitimate and separate entity. That's how you personally insulate yourself from the debts of your business and safeguard your corporate protection.

How should we organize the expanding business?

Here, the best advice is to put your 'eggs' into separate baskets. It's another vital protective strategy. If you use one corporation or LLC to operate one business, then use two separate entities to operate two businesses and so forth. You want to separately incorporate *every* business. If one fails or is sued, it won't then endanger the others. Multi-corporations (or LLCs) limit your losses. You can find corporate graveyards littered with once-thriving companies that vanished because all their 'eggs' were in one corporate basket. Even the smartest entrepreneurs make mistakes and become saddled with losers. Your goal is to isolate your potential losers from your present or future winners. The only way to achieve this is to compartmentalize each venture with a separate corporation or LLC. You can then more easily and safely shed your losers and build on your winners. Operating your expanding business through one entity will give you the advantage of operational simplicity, but we think protection is far more important – particularly when you're small, growing and vulnerable. You can own multi-corporations or LLCs through one holding company, LLC or limited partnership. Each operating corporation or LLC would be a subsidiary. Or if you operate through LLCs, check the Series LLC because each cell within the Series can operate autonomously.

Is it equally wise for liability protection to divide one entity into separate entities?

Of course. It can be smart to divide one corporation or LLC into separate entities. Your objective is to confine the more liability-prone activities to one corporation, and conduct your safer activities and/or title your more valuable assets through another corporation. What's the core of your business? Where and how is your business most likely to incur liability? How can you separate the two? That's how you defensively organize. We review our clients' business organizations. How can we isolate those risky business activities to a separate corporation? How can we restructure their present organization so that one big lawsuit or creditor problem won't cause total organizational failure? But be careful. Separate entities can lose their protection if they don't operate as separate entities. Affiliated companies cannot share bank accounts, commingle cash, inventory or other assets, use one payroll account, combine corporate meetings, or generally operate as one large entity. If one entity goes bankrupt, its creditors can force its affiliates into bankruptcy and claim their combined assets. It's more cumbersome to run separate businesses, but the effort is vital, particularly in these litigious times.

What if a business owns a building or other valuable assets? How can these assets be protected if the business fails or is sued?

That is another important point. The goal of the business owners should be to title as few valuable assets as possible to their operating company. Why needlessly lose valuable assets if their business fails or is sued? It's smarter to title these more valuable assets to another entity to isolate them from the business' creditors. These assets owned through another entity can then be leased or licensed to the operating company.

For example, we always title our clients' real estate separately. For instance, if your building is titled to your business' corporation or LLC, the business' creditors can then claim the building as a corporate asset. So why expose the real estate? It's smarter to title the real estate to a separate limited liability company. The real estate then remains yours, no matter what happens to your business. Similarly, you want to title equipment, furniture and fixtures, trademarks, trade names, copyrights, patents, domain addresses and other proprietary rights to separate entities and then lease or license these assets back to your operating company. Your objective is to limit the business' creditors to the fewest and least valuable assets. You can then sell or use these valuable and protected assets to start another business or for your personal profit. In any instance, they won't be lost to your business' creditors. That's smart planning. But it takes foresight and a defensive mindset.

Can someone also protect their business's lease if a business fails?

Its location may be a business' most important asset. That is the case for many businesses. So a good lease needs special protection. The strategy is not to have the operating business directly hold the lease. If it directly holds the lease, the bankruptcy court can transfer the lease to a buyer. If you lose your lease, you lose your business. But there are several ways to protect a lease. One solution is to hold the lease through another entity and have the landlord consent to allow you to assign or sublet the lease and location to your operating company as a tenant-at-will. You would then continue

155

to control the location if your business fails. For example, you might evict your failing business and sublet the space to a successor business that you'd own at the same location – under a new sublet agreement. Or the landlord can permit you to pledge or assign your lease as collateral security to a friendly mortgage holder. If your business fails, that friendly mortgage holder can then rent the space to your successor business or to any other business that you designate.

You explained how equity reduction mortgages can shield the family home and investment properties. Can this also work for a business?

For a creditor proof business, look for the silver lining in any mortgage that can shield your business' assets from less friendly creditors. Creditors don't want assets fully mortgaged to another creditor. The challenge is to find that friendly creditor to debt-shield your business. Consider the possibilities. Did a relative loan you money to begin or expand the business? Perhaps you loaned money to your business. Why not secure it with a mortgage? Do you owe a friendly supplier? Why not give this supplier a mortgage on your business to help keep other wolves at bay? A friendly banker or another lender may also be helpful if that lender would cooperate. A friendly lender can save your business during the tough times. They also give you the shield you need to discourage lawsuits.

How can you equity-strip a business with a collateralized loan when its credit is poor, its assets have questionable value, or the business cannot afford the interest payments?

Few businesses can completely encumber their assets through conventional commercial loans. They may have poor credit or too little cash flow for interest payments. And in today's economy, getting loans is indeed difficult. Fortunately, other obligations – as well as cash loans – can serve as the basis for a lien. Liens are commonly used to secure all types of obligations in the normal course of business, and these liens are every bit as valid as cash loans. Furthermore, a lien securing an executory obligation may be more advantageous in some ways over a lien securing a cash loan. For example, there is generally no negative tax or economic consequence from fulfilling or failing to fulfill an executory obligation. You may also have no immediate interest expense. We might structure a security agreement so that the lien is not reduced or paid down until the obligation is fully completed. We can even structure the agreement so that the lien amount increases until the obligation is fulfilled. The secured obligation ensures that the asset never has value to other creditors. Moreover, if your business doesn't have the cash to pay down a conventional loan, your 'protected' property will then be in danger of foreclosure. However, cash shortages won't affect your ability to fulfill non-monetary obligations, (or rather you could arrange a monetary obligation with a 'friendly' entity) so foreclosure wouldn't be a problem. Nor need you worry about how you'll get $500,000 to equity-strip a $500,000 business. Cash loans are quantifiable. You can't get a 'large' lien to secure a small loan. However, certain obligations are difficult to quantify. You then have far greater leeway to structure an obligation of 'equivalent value' to the cash value of the lien. How then can you create a bona fide obligation to justify a valid lien on your business or other property?

One advanced and innovative method to equity-strip a business, or any other asset, is through the LLC capitalization technique. Two parties would form a limited liability company (LLC) to run a business, whether to consult or to invest. Each member can obligate the other, per written agreement, to contribute capital (assets) to the company so that it has funds to operate. One member contributes a smaller amount of assets up front to capitalize the company. This would be in exchange for a small ownership interest (usually 1-5 percent). The other member promises to make a large capital contribution over time in exchange for an upfront majority ownership interest in the company (95-99 percent). Because the first member contributed his capital up front, and the second member contributed nothing – the LLC liens the second member's property to ensure that the second member fulfills his obligation to capitalize the LLC over time. As long as the LLC is not considered an 'insider' under applicable fraudulent transfer law, the obligation is valid, its fulfillment demonstrable, and the transaction 'makes sense' in a business context, you can create a rock-solid lien against the second member's property or business to secure the executory obligation. Again, the 'devil is in the details'. It must be properly structured so it's not seen as a sham on the courts or creditors. This takes sophisticated planning.

There are other examples. Lease agreements often contain a lessor's lien clause. These liens are not part of an intentional asset protection program; still these liens arise in the normal course of business. The lessor wants to make sure that the lessee fulfills his lease obligations. The lessor then encumbers the lessee's accounts receivable, furniture, equipment, inventory and other assets. Of course, in this situation, the lessor isn't actually trying to protect the lessee's assets against other creditors, yet that is exactly what the lessor is accomplishing. The best type of lessor's lien, of course, is one held by a friendly lessor. You can then draft the lease and lien terms that best suits your needs.

You have other options. For example, you may sell property from one business to another business and lease it back to the original business. This 'lease-back' arrangement has two benefits: You protect the property by titling it to a separate entity, and when you lease the property back to the original entity, you can place a lessor's lien on a second asset. For example, an LLC could sell an office building to a second LLC, lease the building back to the first LLC and place a lessor's lien on the first LLC's accounts receivable. As simple as the concept appears, a lessor's lien in this or similar circumstances still requires skillful implementation. The goal is to transfer the original asset into a separate entity in a way that it won't be considered a fraudulent transfer.

How can we best protect accounts receivable?

Another valuable business asset can be its accounts receivable. This is true for physicians and other professionals and service providers who may have few tangible assets but considerable receivables. Of course, you can encumber accounts receivable with liens in the same way you can encumber any other asset. For lawsuit protection you can also factor or sell the receivables to a factoring company for fast cash, which is always more easily protected. Factoring companies buy receivables owed by business customers with acceptable credit for a modest discount. Factoring companies specialize. Some buy receivables due to physicians and other professionals, but there are factors for every type business. Your objective is to find your best deal when you want fast cash and less exposed receivables. It's also possible to use receivables to secure insurance premium financing. Essentially, you encumber the receivables and use the premiums to buy life insurance which is ordinarily creditor exempt. This, however, should be reviewed with your professional financial advisor to determine that it makes economic sense.

You can also establish your own accounts receivable billing and collection firm where only the net proceeds after all billing and collection costs would be remitted to the debtor company. The larger share may remain with the billing and collection company as earned fees. You can see that we have many legitimate ways to encumber any size or type business.

How can you secure your own investment in your business?

Money that you loan or invest in your business is money you can easily lose. Your objective here is to reduce or eliminate the risk of losing your own investment in your business and to simultaneously create a defensible mortgage to shield your business.

First, consider the *wrong* way to finance your business. That's to *directly* invest in your business – whether to buy the corporate shares (equity), or as a loan to your business. If your business fails you are then only a stockholder or an unsecured creditor. In either case, you'll reclaim little or none of your investment. However, you can legally secure your investment with the assets of your business. You can then claim priority over claims of other creditors. The key is to have a bank or another lender directly make the loan to your business. Your business would pledge its assets as collateral to the lender. Your lender will lend money to your business because you have pledged enough personal assets to fully collateralize the loan so your lender has no risk. If your business fails, your lender as its secured party would be the *first* creditor repaid from the liquidation. With the lender repaid, it would release whatever personal assets you pledged to the bank as security. Review this plan with your attorney. An investment structured in this manner gives you two advantages: 1) Your investment is better protected; 2) you indirectly control the mortgage against your business and can better protect your business against lawsuits.

Do you have tips to reduce large liability insurance premiums?

Liability insurance for any business or practice can be enormously expensive. But a few cost-cutting strategies can help you buy more insurance protection or pay smaller premiums: 1) Segregate the costs for each type of insurance you now own. You may discover that one type coverage tripled in cost over the years while other coverages have decreased. Which coverage is still a good buy? Which should you reduce or eliminate? 2) Increase your deductibles. Absorb whatever losses you can afford. You'll substantially reduce your premiums. 3) Utilize free programs that cut insurance costs. For instance, insurance companies reduce vehicle insurance premiums by enrolling risky drivers in drivers' education classes. 4) 'Red-line' or distressed area businesses may qualify for federal or government subsidized insurance. Inquire with your state insurance commissioner. 5) Your trade association might deliver substantial savings if you buy the liability insurance they sponsor. 6) Do you own multiple businesses? Buy a package policy. It can reduce your premiums by 25 percent or more. 7) Buy only *vital* insurance. For instance, as your equipment depreciates, lower its coverage. Insurance companies pay only replacement values for lost assets. Excess coverage wastes money. 8) Shop. Insurance rates are regulated in only several states. Once you know the coverage you want, get five bids. Repeat the process annually. Today's lowest costs insurer may be next year's highest.

What about captive insurance companies for professionals and business owners? Can you expand upon them?

We speak to many groups of business owners and professionals about asset protection and tax-favored wealth planning, and we are often asked about international captive insurance companies. 'Captives' or tax-exempt closely held insurance companies (CICs) are useful for both asset protection and tax deferral – provided they are suited to your economic needs, and you qualify for their considerable tax benefits. The CIC is a legitimate insurance company. It is licensed to write insurance in the U.S. and registered with the IRS. Though based in international jurisdictions, international CICs sell more than a third of the total commercial insurance sold within the United States. Many Fortune 500 companies have long used CICs to protect their excess cash, to gain tax advantages, and to lower their own insurance costs. Now individuals, smaller business owners and professionals also take advantage of CICs by setting up their own.

By owning your own CIC, you can insure all or a portion of your business or professional practice from significant risks – such as malpractice or other liabilities or losses for which you would typically carry insurance. By insuring yourself through your own CIC, you get a present year tax deduction on the premiums and you can pay any claims with pre-tax dollars out of the CIC's loss reserves. Your CIC can insure low liability risks, or your CIC can transfer risk to another reinsurer. You would then have little economic risk while enjoying significant tax benefits. Whether you own a CIC as an individual professional, business owner or member of a group you can take a significant deduction each year and grow your funds in the CIC completely tax-free. You can later reclaim the funds and pay only long-term capital gains tax. This three-tier tax advantage is unavailable through pensions, IRAs or other retirement plans.

In addition to its tax benefits, the CIC offers superb asset protection. Your CIC can supplement your existing liability policy. This 'excess' malpractice protection also gives you the security that you won't be wiped out by a lawsuit in excess of your present coverage. Also, the pre-tax premiums paid to your own CIC are protected from the creditors of your business or professional practice. You accomplish all this without losing control of your international funds. If you own a business or professional practice with $400,000 or more in annual profits, consider forming your own captive insurance company.

What's the one most important thing a business can do to avoid liability?

Unquestionably a risk management and liability audit is essential. Companies get sued from employees, customers, suppliers, regulators and just about everyone else. That's why we encourage our business clients to review their policies, procedures, contracts and operations. We want to identify potential problems before they turn into lawsuits. This lawsuit prevention assessment is an increasingly growing part of our business and these audits have greatly reduced the number of lawsuits encountered by our participating clients.

10

Protecting
Other Assets

Let's discuss some other assets one can own and how we can protect these 'miscellaneous' assets.

There are many other assets that range from bank accounts and wage income to life insurance, jewelry, vehicles, intellectual property and even money due from others that you can lose in a lawsuit. These 'miscellaneous' assets are frequently overlooked and unprotected. Everyone should complete a *detailed* inventory of *every* asset that they own. They should then check their state exemption laws. Some of these assets may be partly or fully protected from lawsuits. For example, bankruptcy and state exemption laws oftentimes protect life insurance, annuities, burial plots, tools of the trade, vehicles, wedding rings, wages, child support payments and social security payments. We have already discussed the homestead and retirement account exemptions. You must then, obviously, title miscellaneous assets that have no statutory exemption to one or more protective entities, encumber them with liens or adopt other protective strategies.

Life insurance is oftentimes a major asset. How can you make life insurance become lawsuit-proof?

Life insurance usually enjoys state statutory protection. But again, its protection depends on state laws. Still, if you own a large life insurance policy you may title your insurance policy to an *irrevocable life insurance trust* (ILIT). An ILIT is an irrevocable trust specifically designed to own life insurance. As with other trusts, the ILIT has a trustee, beneficiaries, and terms for distributions. Your ILIT would own your insurance policy and would be the policy beneficiary. When you die, your insurer pays the ILIT trustee who then distributes the proceeds to the ILIT beneficiaries. Your estate shouldn't be the beneficiary, nor should you retain other incidence of ownership.

An ILIT can be unfunded or funded. With an unfunded ILIT, the life insurance premiums are not fully paid. Future premiums are paid to the trustee who then pays the premiums. With a funded ILIT you transfer to the trust either a fully paid insurance policy or enough income-producing assets to pay future premiums. Whether your ILIT is unfunded or funded, the policy premiums must be directly paid from the trust. If you directly pay the premiums you lose the trust's tax benefits and creditor protection. Since the ILIT is irrevocable, it protects the policy's cash value, death proceeds and trust distributions. If life insurance isn't *fully* creditor protected under your state laws, then an ILIT is essential.

As importantly, the ILIT can save you estate taxes because the ILIT – not you personally – owns the life insurance. Therefore, policy proceeds in the trust are not included in your taxable estate. This is why you save estate taxes. To illustrate, if you are single and die with a three million dollar estate which includes a one million dollar life insurance policy, and have a two million dollar death tax exemption; your estate would pay an estate tax on the one million dollars. If we assume an estate tax of about 50 percent, your estate taxes would be about $500,000. An ILIT eliminates the one million dollar life insurance proceeds from your taxable estate. Your estate saves about $500,000 because you reduced your taxable estate to zero. Also, the ILIT gives you greater control over policy distributions. For example, if you personally own your insurance, your insurance will directly go to the named beneficiaries when you die. An ILIT lets you control *how* and *when* the policy proceeds are distributed. Spendthrift, anti-alienation, discretionary distribution and other protective provisions in the trust can further protect the insurance proceeds from your beneficiaries' creditors.

Do you have exposed cash that you do not foreseeably need? It may be smart to buy *more* life insurance. Of course, not everyone needs more life insurance, but life insurance may be a simple way to shield excess cash from creditors because *every* state at least partially creditor protects life insurance. Moreover, it can be a tax efficient way to build your estate, a retirement nest egg or simply a way to leave considerably more money to your beneficiaries.

Annuities and life insurance policies are only exempt in some states. Even in states that protect these assets, they are often only exempt if structured properly. In some states we must not only pay attention to who the policy's insured person, owner and beneficiaries are, but we must also examine the wording of the policy before we can say with any certainty that the policy is exempt. For example, Utah protects life insurance proceeds, but only if the beneficiaries are the insured person's spouse or children. Alabama protects life insurance from the claims of creditors of a policy's beneficiary, but only if the beneficiary is someone other than the insured and the policy states that the proceeds are exempt from creditor attachment. Not surprisingly, many insurance policies don't include such protective language. To further muddy the waters, some states address to what extent cash proceeds are exempt from attachment, and other states don't. If a state is silent on whether proceeds are protected, does that mean the policy is only safe from attachment before it's converted to cash? How long are the proceeds safe after they are received? If statutory law is silent, we must then look to case law, which of course will vary by state. In any case, to be as safe as possible we should never commingle insurance proceeds with other funds. They should be kept in a separate account so that they're clearly identified and thus afforded the maximum protection under law.

Finally, we should consider fraudulent transfer law if planning is done after a creditor threat has already materialized. Some states have adopted fraudulent conversion laws to specifically address whether transforming an exempt asset to a non-exempt asset, such as insurance, in order to avoid creditors is fraudulent. If such a purchase is made after a creditor threat has arisen, the fraudulent conversion law (if a given state has such a law) tends to operate differently than fraudulent transfer law. This means that even if a transfer is not fraudulent under fraudulent transfer law, it may be fraudulent under fraudulent conversion law. Whether a transfer is fraudulent will vary from state to state.

What suggestions do you have on protectively titling autos and other vehicles?

Automobiles, boats and other vehicles are typically not one's most valuable assets, yet vehicles are assets that judgment creditors can quickly and easily seize. One alternative is to title automobiles and other vehicles to the less wealthy spouse, but it's far preferable to title them to a separate entity such as an LLC. This will better protect you against the uninsured accident where someone else (such as a child) causes the accident. For protection, it's usually enough to refinance a vehicle if a judgment is imminent. This leaves no equity for the creditor. Vehicles should *never* be co-owned. For instance, if a husband and wife co-own a car, both spouses will be sued if the vehicle is involved in an accident. Your objective when you title your vehicles is to personally insulate yourself from liabilities caused by the vehicle. Simultaneously, you want to protect your equity in the vehicle from your personal creditors. To accomplish this, one should title their vehicles – including boats and airplanes – to an LLC. We also recommend that our clients purchase a one million dollar liability policy and a two million dollar umbrella policy. Liens against your vehicles can complete its protection, as can leasing your vehicle.

How should antiques and other collectibles be titled?

Most states partly protect household furniture from creditor claims. Again, you must check your state exemptions. The new Bankruptcy Act also protects furnishings to a modest value. Moreover, ordinary household furniture has little resale value and is seldom seized by creditors. On the other hand, more valuable antiques, heirlooms, art, pianos, electronics, jewelry and valuable collections (stamps, coins, etc.) need protection. One obvious alternative is to sell or pawn your exposed personal assets and spend or protect the cash proceeds, if creditor seizure is imminent. Or you may transfer these assets to a family limited partnership, particularly if these assets will increase in value and can be viewed as an investment. Still, another alternative is to exchange any exposed assets with your spouse for exempt assets of equal value. Finally, you may also pledge these assets as collateral for loans.

What wages can a creditor garnish and how can they be protected?

The portion of your paycheck a creditor can garnish is limited by both federal and state laws. As with any other state exemption, each state set its own wage protection limitations. Some states completely exempt wages from creditor garnishment, particularly those earned by the 'head-of-the-household'. New York, for example, shelters 90 percent of a debtor's net wages. Only 10 percent in aggregate can be claimed by a debtor's creditors. But as with the homestead laws, to protect your wages, you must follow your state laws. For instance, your state may require that you segregate your wages in a 'wage exemption' or 'wage earner' account. Wages commingled with unprotected funds lose their protection. Your wages are also protected under federal law. The federal Consumer Credit Protection Act (CCPA) limits wage garnishment to the lesser of: 1) 25 percent of the debtor's disposable income per week (*disposable income* is the net paycheck after deducting federal and state withholding and FICA taxes); or 2) the amount by which a weekly disposable income exceeds 30 times the federal minimum hourly wage. Nor can exempt or protected wages be garnished by your creditor once you receive it, provided you keep the wages segregated from your non-wage funds. However, commissions, royalties, rents, fees and other forms of income may not fall within the wage exemption definition.

One option to shelter your wages is to form a corporation and direct your wages to the corporation. For tax purposes, you can withdraw the money as loans. This simple strategy is sometimes used by debtors to temporarily shield non-exempt wages from creditors; however it isn't a practical long-term solution. Moreover, your employer must be willing to treat your corporation as an independent contractor, and, understandably, few employers will agree to this. Another wage protection strategy is to make a prior wage assignment to a 'friendlier' creditor who then periodically 'loans' you money. Wage assignments must be in writing and in effect prior to the creditor's garnishment. As a practical matter, wage garnishments are usually not a prolonged problem. Most debtors under a wage garnishment, settle their case, file bankruptcy, or simply stop working.

There are several exceptions to the wage exemption laws. For instance, the Child Support Enforcement Act of 1975 overrides federal and state income exemptions for purposes of allowing a spouse to enforce alimony or child support orders. Alimony and child support payments are generally not exempt from garnishment by either the payer's or recipient's creditors. Support payments in some states have a limited exemption. Another exception is an IRS wage garnishment.

What other forms of income aren't sheltered from garnishment and how can they be sheltered?

Welfare payments are usually exempt from creditor claims; but again, the state laws on this are not uniform. Some states partially protect welfare payments, others provide no protection. Public assistance programs (Aid to Families with Dependent Children or AFDC) are protected in some states. Welfare payments lose their protection once they're received and commingled with non-welfare funds. Public assistance payments – such as aid to the blind and aid to the elderly and disabled – are generally protected by state law. The proceeds from the sale or financing of exempt assets that are used to acquire non-exempt assets also lose their protection.

Social Security and disability income payments aren't lawsuit-proof. Social Security is not considered a pension under the Employee Retirement Income Security Act (ERISA) and therefore is not federally protected. A creditor's right to garnish Social Security checks depends entirely upon state law. Bankruptcy or encumbering these monies due to you are the two best solutions.

Has the new bankruptcy law extended protection for certain types of income?

Yes. The new bankruptcy laws now fully protects: 1) Social Security benefits, unemployment compensation and local public assistance payments; 2) veterans' benefits; 3) disability, illness and unemployment benefits; 4) payments under a stock bonus, pension or profit sharing plan, annuity or similar plan on account of illness. Of course, to claim the bankruptcy exemption, you must file bankruptcy otherwise your state law governs their protection and your state protection may be inadequate. But bankruptcy can be your right option when you anticipate future income from these sources which lack state protection.

How can notes receivable or other monies due to me from third parties be shielded if I am sued?

One alternative is to sell your receivables to a factor that will purchase the receivables at a discounted price. You can also sell mortgages or other notes due to you, as well as judgments or other claims against third parties. Or you might accelerate payment of the receivable by offering an attractive discount. You can certainly more easily protect cash than you can money due you on a note. Generally, we title notes, mortgages, structured settlements and other significant future monies due to a client to a limited partnership. We may also pledge the note as collateral security to a more friendly creditor to equity-strip it.

How can a large bank account be protectively titled?

Large bank accounts, in our view, should be titled to a limited partnership – and preferably in an account in another state. We protect more substantial accounts (usually over $500,000) in international trusts or international LLCs. Or larger accounts can be titled to limited partnerships, which in turn would be owned by an international trust. In some states, spouses – with some level of safety – can title their accounts as tenants-by-the-entirety. There are other options to protect cash accounts from creditors. For example, you may 'sprinkle' gifts. This will also reduce your estate taxes. Or you may pay down loans against exempt assets – such as mortgages against a fully homesteaded home. But there are other options. One may, for example, buy exempt assets, pay preferred creditors or non-dischargeable debts (student loans, fines or taxes), or prepay future expenses. There are many ways to rapidly and legally deplete bank accounts in the face of a lawsuit.

What about safe deposit boxes? Is there a better option than to rent one in your own name?

Creditors sometimes check the ownership and contents of safe deposit boxes. If your box contains anything worthwhile, don't keep the safe deposit box in your own name. It's best to rent it instead through a corporation or LLC. For more privacy, one shouldn't be the officer or manager of the entity. Nominee firms are available for this purpose. Also don't hold the key to the safe deposit box as creditors invariably ask about this.

Are 529 accounts for a child's college tuition safe from creditors?

The answer here depends largely on state law. But even when these accounts are fully protected, they are only safe if the transfer of funds to the account is a completed gift and the account is properly titled as a custodial account under the child's Social Security number. The same holds true with other transfers under the Uniform Gift to Minors Act (UGTMA). Transfers to these accounts, however, may be recovered as fraudulent.

Finally, what about valuable technology patents, trademarks and other intellectual property? What protective entity best protects them?

For many people – and particularly businesses – their patents, trademarks, copyrights, domain addresses, customer lists, formulas and other intellectual property are their most important and valuable assets. We have our clients title these accounts to one or more LLCs or LPs, and then license the rights to use these assets to one or more of their operating companies. It's never wise to directly title these valuable assets to your operating company or to yourself personally as these assets can then be lost if you or your business are successfully sued. Our preference is to use a Nevis or Cook Island LLC to hold intellectual property. These international entities not only creditor shelter these assets but insure privacy not available through domestic entities.

11

Protecting Your Assets In Different Situations

Thank you for explaining how one may shield their various assets. Let's finally discuss the protective strategies one can take against the different type claims that may jeopardize their wealth.

You said earlier that how one best protects their assets depends largely on the nature of the financial threat. Can you expand upon this?

Absolutely! Divorce, creditors, lawsuits and property foreclosures are all potential dangers to one's wealth. Each type claim demands its own wealth protection strategy. As the financial professional protects their clients against various types of investment and economic threats, we must protect our clients from a wide variety of predatory threats. But there is no one 'cookie-cutter' strategy that is best against all threats.

Aside from lawsuits, what are the most common predatory threats?

Divorces are rapidly escalating in numbers. Many of our clients come to us for assistance on this matter. Of course, the bad economy has created serious financial problems for many of our clients who now have general creditor issues.

I imagine that most of your clients are concerned about lawsuits as opposed to say, divorce.

That's true. About 90 percent of our clients are either involved in litigation or foresee the potential for future litigation. And they worry for good reason. About one in four adult Americans are sued each year and the number of lawsuits continues to escalate. That's why we repeatedly say that asset protection is a vital part of financial planning. It's not enough just to make money. You have to work even harder to protect it!

Who's responsible for the lawsuit explosion?

There's no simple answer to this. But clearly too many people look at litigation as a way to easily obtain money and get rich quick. Too many lawyers in this country also feed the lawsuit frenzy. Watch TV. Read the newspapers. Notice the billboards. There's always some lawyer pitching their services to sue someone. And that someone can be *you*!

We would imagine that professionals – such as doctors – are the prime lawsuit targets.

That's no longer true. Our client base includes people from virtually every occupation. Real estate owners, small business owners, employers, corporate officers and directors, financial and investment advisors, celebrities and sports figures, accountants and even other lawyers all come to us for protection. We really have an exceptionally broad client base.

If a client is sued, do they always have to defend against the lawsuit?

We always advise our clients to defend the case unless the client is an obvious bankruptcy candidate because he or she has so many other creditors or lawsuits. But if you are victimized by only one lawsuit, why do nothing and give the plaintiff a default judgment? Defending a lawsuit is expensive, time consuming and emotionally draining, but we have found that most plaintiffs will settle for comparatively little – and will settle early – once they learn that our client is well-fortified. But we always want the opposition to know that they will be in for a fight if they don't settle. After all, they also have lawyers to pay.

I imagine that legal fees in defending a lawsuit can impoverish your clients?

It happens. That's why we try to avoid litigation with early settlements. And, yes, we do have clients who come to our office after spending hundreds of thousands of dollars in legal fees. Sometimes the parties spend far more in litigation costs than what the subject of the controversy is about. Still, the trial lawyers are happy to run-up-the-clock. Too few lawyers look for ways to save their clients legal fees. In fact, legal fees have increased by 57 percent in the last 5 years. And jokes about lawyers billing 62 hours in a single day are no longer a laughing matter – not when you're paying the bill.

Does your firm defend lawsuits against your clients?

No. We focus on asset protection and integrated estate planning. We do not do trial work. However, we do, wherever necessary, coordinate our services with the client's defense counsel and quite often participate in settlement negotiations. We also, where necessary, assist clients in finding good defense counsel to represent them, and we work with quite a number of defense attorneys from throughout the country who can economically and professionally handle a client's case. If one of our asset protection plans is challenged then, of course, we actively participate in defending the plan.

Can a plaintiff attack a defendant's property before the plaintiff wins a judgment – or even serves the lawsuit on the defendant?

Possibly. Depending on the specific case and the practices of the defendant's state courts, a party suing may be able to attach your real estate, bank accounts or personal property before proving their case at trial. This may be accomplished by filing a court approved lien, a lis pendens (against real estate) or an attachment of bank accounts and personal property. The court may also issue a freeze order or injunction restraining the defendant or other third parties from transferring or dissipating assets pending the trial. Pre-judgment attachments are most common in divorce cases. They are far less common with routine civil cases.

Is it too late to protect yourself after you are sued?

Not necessarily, but you'll find it more difficult to do so and you'll have fewer protective options once you are sued. Moreover, it may be too late in the sense that your assets may already be attached. As we said earlier, you then also have to be more mindful of the fraudulent transfer laws or the possibility that the court may unwind your plan. Still, a defendant to a lawsuit has the absolute right to attempt to shield his or her assets, even after a lawsuit has commenced.

In your view, what are the most common mistakes clients make when confronted with a lawsuit?

That's a great question. We can offer a number of observations. First is the tendency to panic over a significant lawsuit. We well-understand our clients' fears, nevertheless most lawsuits do end up without major loss to the client. Again, much of our role is to play psychologist and calm our clients' worries. Of course, we can more effectively do this only if we had protected his or her assets.

175

The second common error is to spend too much on legal fees to defend the case. A successful outcome depends on minimizing your legal fees. Few clients manage their lawyer's fees properly.

Thirdly, is the failure of the client – and his attorney – to make certain the client's assets are well-protected – and to use that protection as a lever to favorably settle the case *before* the legal fees mount.

We suppose the axiom is true that "once you are sued you automatically lose". So the fourth error is the failure to quash conflicts before they become full-blown lawsuits. Then, only the lawyers win.

Can a plaintiff ask a defendant about their assets before they win a judgment?

Not normally, and the reason is because the defendant's financial affairs only relates to the collectability on a judgment and usually has nothing to do with the merits of a case. But there are exceptions – as in fraudulent transfer cases where the movement of assets is the heart of the case. Another instance where it is permitted is when the plaintiff is suing for punitive damages. Then the defendant's net worth is relevant to the amount that would be considered appropriately punitive.

What is the best defense to a lawsuit?

A strong offense is the best defense! More important than an inexpensive lawyer is the lawyer who can and will fight like a tiger. Your lawyer must counterpunch. Make it painful for the plaintiff to sue...or continue the fight. Can you counterclaim? Who else can you drag into the fray? Can you swamp your adversary with discovery? Can you depose others who your adversary wouldn't want involved? Can you raise embarrassing facts that your opponent wants buried? Is your lawyer clever enough to run up your adversary's legal fees while holding down your own? You can't be a punching bag. You must throw a few right hooks yourself. Put on your own boxing gloves! Oftentimes the best thing a defendant can do is to drop their unaggressive lawyer for one who knows how to throw a few tough punches.

We talked about huge legal fees. Do you have tips to hold down lawyers' bills?

Whether you win or lose a case, expect huge legal bills. America is one of a few countries where a successful defendant pays his own legal fees and costs. England, and most other countries whose legal systems are similar to our own, has the loser pay the victor's legal fees. In America, each party pays its own fees and costs, unless a contract or special statute says otherwise. You can 'win' your lawsuit and still owe thousands or even millions in legal fees and costs. This is no victory! And legal fees are skyrocketing. Lawyer overbilling is alarmingly rampant. You can try to keep your assets safe from your adversary yet lose a big slice of your wealth to your own lawyer. You must limit your legal costs *before* you do battle or you'll lose the war even if you win in court.

Avoid big name lawyers. Every community has a lawyer or two reputed to be the best hired guns in town. But few attorneys with golden reputations are worth their excessively steep fees, particularly when a junior associate will handle much of your case. Hire an attorney experienced with your type case, a lawyer who'll respect your need for an economical, fast, and relatively painless resolution. Also shorten the battle. Lawyers can needlessly prolong any case. Endless depositions and court appearances are tactics that only generate horrendous legal bills. You seldom get a corresponding benefit. Watch your lawyer's clock. You largely control your legal costs if you control your demands on your attorney. Still, lawyers pad their bills, churn needless work and mount billable hours. Non-lawyers can't easily determine what fees are reasonable. If you're in doubt, let an impartial lawyer review the legal services and the fee. The opinion should come from someone who can objectively assess the services and fees without a stake in what you'll do with that advice. Finally, talk honestly with your lawyer if you feel overcharged. If you still are unsatisfied, arbitrate the fee through the state bar fee arbitration committee.

Aren't there other litigation costs to contend with?

Certainly. If you lose a lawsuit, you'll owe more than what the judge or jury awards the plaintiff. You'll also owe interest on the award. Interest starts from the day the lawsuit is filed. Civil trials can end years after the lawsuit is filed. You'll then owe years of interest, plus the awarded amount. Interest rates vary by state, but range between 5 percent and 18 percent annually. If your state imposes a 12 percent interest (about average) and you're liable for $50,000, after five years of litigation you'll owe $38,000 in interest – or a total of $88,000! Add legal fees, witness expenses, court costs, transcripts and the time you spend not making money and you can see litigation's true cost. Consider these economics when you negotiate settlement. Minor lawsuits can end up literally bankrupting defendants.

What are your views on mediation and arbitration?

Litigation is expensive, cumbersome and time-consuming. That's why alternate dispute resolution (ADR) mediation or arbitration is fast replacing the courtroom battle. A mediator opens communication and encourages settlement. Arbitration makes final binding awards. Testimony is presented at a hearing overseen by an arbitrator who arbitrates under American Arbitration Association rules.

Nearly every civil case today goes through mandatory mediation because the courts want to settle as many cases as possible. Certain cases require arbitration by statute, but usually the parties agree to binding arbitration within their original contract. However, you can agree to arbitrate once a dispute arises.

Arbitration isn't always preferable for a defendant because arbitration moves rapidly. Litigation can be prolonged for years. Time is always a bargaining chip for the defendant. On the other hand, arbitration can lower your legal fees, avoid punitive damage awards, and put your case before a panel of arbitrators. They are likely to render a fairer verdict than a jury.

How do plaintiffs collect on their judgments?

A judgment creditor seizes your assets by *executing on their judgment*. The specific processes vary by state, but typically, for real property, the creditor files a summary of judgment in the county recorder where your real property is located. This 'liens' the property to the amount of the judgment. This lien is valid against any real property owned in your own name in that county at the time, as well as any future acquired real estate. You can't sell or refinance liened property without satisfying the judgment. Thus, a lien effectively ties up your real estate until you pay the judgment and/or settle.

Personal property is seized through levy. The Sheriff or Marshall physically takes the property described in the levy, whether directly from you or from a third party. This includes money in bank accounts, items in your safe deposit box, automobiles, jewelry, antiques, collectibles, equipment, or any other unprotected physical assets. The sheriff converts property to cash through a sheriff's public auction.

Wages are seized by a levy or garnishment. The creditor's levy orders your employer to send your pay to the creditor (except for the legally protected exemption).

If a creditor is about to take your assets or garnish your wages, you must immediately take three steps to protect yourself. First, file a claim of exemption to protect your exempt assets. Each state lists assets a creditor cannot take. This includes tools of the trade, household items and specified personal property. Federal law provides further exemptions. You'll need to file a claim of exemption to properly shield this exempt property. Their protection is not automatic. Second, pay the judgment or settle; perhaps you'll pay over time. Negotiating settlement saves the creditor foreclosure hassles and you get to keep your property. Your third option, file Chapter 7, 11 or 13 bankruptcy *before* the auction. Bankruptcy has serious consequences, but it will stop a forced sale of your assets. If you plan bankruptcy, do it *before* seizure and sale to save your assets.

We talked about liability insurance, but let's expand upon this. What's your view about liability insurance for risk management?

Generally, we are all for it. But you need enough insurance. Too little coverage will still expose you to a judgment in excess of your coverage. And a good plaintiff's lawyer can manipulate a jury to make an outlandish award far beyond your policy limits.

You can't predict what you can lose once you are sued. Years ago we could, with reasonable accuracy, predict the outcome of a lawsuit. Juries were sane. Judges cut excessive awards. Punitive damage claims that awarded a plaintiff millions for no damages were unheard of. That was then. The courts compensated actual losses. Not today. Courtrooms now redistribute wealth. You can't be confident that your million-dollar policy is *enough*. No matter how much liability insurance you carry, some litigant will sue you for more.

Most cases do settle within the policy limits. But until that happens, you will anguish that possibly you will be hit with a judgment that will *exceed* your coverage. You will then lose your assets despite your insurance. You will also have to hire your own lawyer to defend yourself against your potential excess liability.

So how much liability insurance is enough? That's a tough question to answer. If insurance were free, we would say to buy all you can. But insurance isn't free. The more you buy the more you pay. You must then balance the cost of increased coverage against the risks from less coverage. You must not only consider the probability of an excess judgment against you but also what you could lose if you did face a judgment beyond your policy limits. Since you can never buy enough coverage to insulate yourself against today's insatiable litigation demands, your only solution is to also protect yourself by means other than insurance.

Doesn't liability insurance actually encourage lawsuits?

Absolutely. That's the downside with insurance. Liability insurance is the major impetus behind many costly and frivolous lawsuits. When you are well-insured, you have deep pockets. This can only attract lawsuits. Whether you are rich or poor, a prospective litigant knows that your insurance company has tons of money. Plaintiffs' lawyers know that insurers will settle even a frivolous lawsuit rather than fight, because it is less costly. It is insurance that has greatly contributed to our transformation into a nation of litigants.

Because insurance attracts lawsuits, and because of fast-rising insurance costs, more and more professionals and businesspeople now 'go bare' without insurance. Going bare is particularly common with physicians who have been hardest hit by malpractice suits and exorbitant malpractice premiums. High-risk specialists, obstetricians, orthopedic surgeons, and others pay $100,000 or more annually for their malpractice coverage. Physicians in the litigious states of California, New York, and Florida pay two or three times that for the same coverage. A general practitioner in a low litigation state still pays $20,000 or more annually for insurance. And this won't buy much coverage.

Insurance costs dig deeply into every medical professional's earnings already hammered by reimbursement cutbacks and managed care programs. Nor are unaffordable premiums only a doctor's problem. The litigation explosion has impacted every profession and business. Going bare is gaining traction in even such lower risk occupations as law, financial services, and architecture.

Premium costs are only one reason so many professional and business owners are abandoning insurance. Doctors, other high-risk professionals, and business owners understand that they greatly increase their chances of getting sued only because they are insured. Without liability insurance they wouldn't be deep pocket defendants, particularly if their assets were well-protected.

We have scores of doctor clients who now practice without liability insurance. However, you can't always avoid insurance. Physicians, by state regulation, often must carry malpractice insurance. HMOs and hospitals frequently require their affiliated doctors to carry liability insurance. Most other professionals consider insurance an option. However, going bare can only make sense if you have few assets or if your assets are well-protected.

Going bare discourages lawsuits. We can illustrate this with the case of a cosmetic surgeon who was threatened with five malpractice suits in three years (not one case had apparent merit). In each case we pointed out to the patient's attorney that our doctor client had no insurance and that his assets were protected. Not one patient sued. If this doctor had insurance, he would undoubtedly have been sued several times.

One dilemma of going bare is that you must pay your own defense costs or face a default judgment if you don't defend the case. This quandary is particularly undesirable when you know that you have done nothing wrong. Nor do defense costs come cheap. It can cost $100,000 or more to defend against even a routine liability or malpractice suit.

One compromise solution is to retain a law firm to defend you if you are sued. Your annual retainer would cover the litigation costs. A number of professional and business clients retain us to keep them completely judgment-proof (we continuously monitor their finances to make certain they stay fully protected). These professionals have their defense costs covered through a malpractice defense firm whose fee is paid through a separate defense-only policy. These professionals practice with confidence that they won't lose their assets even if they are sued and lose. Of course, the uninsured professional or business owner should let their clients know that they have no coverage so their client or patient will have dampened enthusiasm to sue.

More legal defense fund insurers are popping up. They insure only the defense costs. But when you couple good legal defense coverage with a good asset protection plan, you may have a smart alternative to huge insurance premiums and an insurance policy that will only magnetize lawsuits.

Still, self-insurance isn't for everybody. Your insurance premiums may be a bargain, considering your risks. Or you may prefer insurance – if only for your own peace of mind. Some people aren't comfortable unless they are insured against every possible lawsuit, no matter how remote the odds. You must assess your own comfort level to decide your best alternative.

When can an employee rely upon an employer's liability coverage?

Contrary to assumption, your employer's insurance also may not adequately protect you. For example, an employer's insurer may not be obliged to defend or pay a judgment against the employee. Employers ordinarily and automatically share liability with their negligent employee; therefore, a judgment against the employee usually brings a simultaneous judgment against the employer. The employer's liability would be paid by the insurer, which would normally cover the employee. That's the theory. Nevertheless, employees who rely solely on their employer's coverage run several risks.

One risk is that you have no protection if your employer is not liable for an error or omission that occurred outside the scope of employment. Or you lose your protection if your employer's policy is terminated without your knowledge. Or your employer may have inadequate insurance. Or too many employees may be sued on the same claim (as is often the case) and the shared liability limits are too low. Or your employer's plan may be a claims-made policy that will cover you only for claims made during the policy period. But you may change jobs *before* a lawsuit is filed. Or lose your job. If you are sued *after* your employment ends, you then have no coverage. That's why we urge our clients to review their employer's policy. Your employer's insurer must defend and protect you and your employer. Evaluate your employer's financial stability. A company in financial difficulty may lose, reduce or cancel their insurance. That's why every employee should buy their own supplemental insurance. It's inexpensive and essential.

Isn't it also true that an insurer may refuse coverage on a particular claim? How often does this happen?

It happens all the time. People who believe that they are insured against a certain claim are always surprised when their insurance company points out their ominous fine print exclusion. For example, one client was sued for $500,000 resulting from his teenage daughter's car accident. He assumed that his auto insurance policy would cover the accident until his insurance agent notified him that his policy didn't cover his daughter because she had moved out of his house to attend college. He paid over $150,000 to settle. You too have endless ways to get into trouble, and your insurance won't always come to your rescue. We repeat: *Buy insurance but don't rely upon it.*

If you are sued and you have liability insurance, keep your insurer on the hook. Your insurer must defend you in good faith or you can sue them for any judgment against you above your coverage. Your insurer can have liability for excessive awards unless it notifies you of the excess claim and settles or attempts to settle the claim in good faith within the policy limits. Your insurer can't refuse a reasonable settlement which exposes you to liability above your insurance. Insurance companies decline claims coverage, but if you question your coverage, demand that your insurance company defend and indemnify you. Your insurer may then defend the claim and reserve the right not to pay any award, or your insurer may litigate its liability under your policy. If you have potential exposure beyond your insurance coverage, hire your own attorney to protect you against an excessive award.

A similar problem with liability insurance is that you lose control over your case. Your insurance company decides whether to settle, and for how much. Perhaps this is unimportant with an automobile accident, but it can be enormously important to you if the lawsuit involves your professional competence or impacts upon your personal reputation.

For example, a doctor may be convinced that he is in the right and wants his day in court. However, his insurance company may consider it cheaper to settle. Or you may want to quickly settle your case to avoid adverse publicity while your insurer insists that your case goes to trial. You and your insurer can have different agendas. If

184

you force your insurance company to resolve your case as you want, you can forfeit the insurance protection for which you paid hefty premiums. And once you are sued, your premiums will rise. With multiple lawsuits over your lifetime – win or lose – your insurance premiums will increase. One physician relied on her malpractice insurance for years until her insurance company defended her on four lawsuits. They hiked her premiums to $250,000 a year. She pays more for her insurance than she would likely pay on any one lawsuit. This isn't unusual.

Divorce is a special type of litigation. How important is asset protection when planning marriage?

It's critical, particularly if you marry with significant wealth and your assets greatly exceed your new spouse's. And this frequently happens because more people are in their second or third marriages or marry later in life when they had already accumulated assets. Divorce can be emotionally and economically devastating and can also be one of life's biggest financial catastrophes. Nor can we forget that marriage is less and less a lifelong commitment. One in two marriages ends in divorce, so asset protection planning is essential whether you are anticipating marriage, happily married, separated, divorcing or have 'problem' ex-spouses.

What are the best ways to financially protect your assets against divorce?

Unquestionably, a fair, legally-binding pre-marriage agreement is your safest way to secure your assets. A pre-marriage agreement is a written contract between intended spouses which specifies how their marital property and income shall be divided should they divorce. And contrary to belief, pre-marriage agreements aren't only for the wealthy. More couples with average income and wealth now use pre-marriage agreements as an efficient, equitable way to settle matters in advance of a future divorce. Pre-marriage agreements also resolve complex issues that are less easily reconciled by a divorce court. For example, a spouse with substantial assets may want his children from a prior marriage to inherit his wealth. A pre-marriage agreement is then the ideal way – perhaps only way – to secure this wish. The pre-marriage agreement can similarly stipulate to a predetermined spousal alimony as well as property division upon separation, divorce or death. The agreement lets both parties marry confident that their respective post-marital needs will be fulfilled should their marriage end. Pre-marriage agreements are particularly useful when the parties don't rely upon each other financially. Older couples often marry for companionship, not financial security. When one or both spouses have wealth and children from a prior marriage, the pre-marriage agreement insures the desired disposition of their respective assets. These couples usually agree to share assets accumulated during their marriage, while assets accumulated before marriage or through inheritance remain their separate property. A pre-marriage agreement promotes fairness, avoids hostility, saves legal fees and divorce court delays and encourages the couples to more predictably plan their financial future.

What if an intended spouse won't sign a pre-marriage agreement? What then is the best option to shield your wealth?

Titling your assets to an international irrevocable trust before you marry is the best option. Irrevocable international trusts can be effective for divorce protection because you no longer own the trust assets and have retained no benefit of ownership. Since you neither own nor control the property, an ex-spouse cannot claim the property.

Can a limited partnership or LLC effectively 'divorce-proof' my assets?

Family limited partnerships (FLPs), limited liability companies (LLCs) and corporations might be useful to help you control certain assets if you divorce. If you set up the entity and transfer your assets to the entity during the marriage, and assume control of the entity as the FLP's sole general partner; the LLC's sole manager; or the corporation's sole officer. Even if the ownership is divided equally, you retain control.

Divorce courts generally don't dissolve FLPs, LLCs or corporations, particularly if third parties – such as children – have an ownership interest. The courts adjust the ownership interests so each ex-spouse winds up with an equal percentage. But if you controlled the entity before the marriage, you should continue in control after you divorce. Nevertheless, in divorce you can still lose a considerable share of your equity in the entity.

Are post-nuptial agreements for spouses helpful?

Sometimes it's a good idea for spouses to negotiate *post-nuptial* agreements. Though married couples can legally contract, they cannot bargain away the same rights that they could under a pre-marriage agreement. Nor do all courts enforce post-nuptial contracts. As with the pre-marriage agreement, a post-nuptial agreement must be fair, both spouses must fully understand the agreement, neither party can defraud the other, and each party should have their own legal counsel. If these conditions are met, the agreement should then stand. Post-nuptial property agreements also cover narrower terms than pre-marriage agreements and they usually specify only what property each spouses will each keep in the event they divorce. We consider post-nuptial agreements particularly valuable to solve the always thorny issue of valuing or apportioning business ownerships in divorce. The business is often the central obstacle to settlement negotiations. Alimony may also be another point resolved through the agreement.

Can assets be divorce-proofed by transferring them internationally?

Sometimes spouses planning divorce do shelter their assets in international asset protection trusts. Although they must disclose these trust assets to the divorce court, the court generally cannot recover or divide these trust assets under divorce. But this hardly assures victory. Divorce courts can award the victimized spouse a greater share of the U.S.-based assets to compensate for the trust-shielded assets. The court might also award the injured spouse compensatory alimony. However, the international trust can effectively secure separate property when you have few or no remaining assets within the United States and your income is too low for the court to even the score through a larger alimony award.

If the family assets are titled to a spouse who is likely to incur liability, are these assets lost to that spouse in divorce?

A common, simple asset protection strategy is to title marital assets with the less-vulnerable spouse. This spouse then controls the assets and can sell, encumber or conceal the entrusted assets. That's one reason why titling marital assets with one spouse is poor planning. Spouses should jointly control marital assets. For asset protection they might, for example, hold title as tenants-by-the-entirety or as general partners in a family limited partnership. If only one spouse has title to the assets, the other spouse should, at the minimum, encumber or escrow the assets to some third party or nominee entity, to prevent the sale or encumbrance of the property. Most state divorce courts equitably divide marital assets notwithstanding which spouse they are titled to.

How do divorce courts divide assets in divorce?

Divorce courts divide property either as equitable distributions or as community property. Courts in equitable distribution states have the discretion to divide whatever property is owned by both spouses. The courts consider the length of the marriage, the age, health, conduct, occupations, skills, and employment and earnings potential of the respective spouses, and other requisite factors included in their state divorce statutes. *Equitable* division doesn't necessarily mean *equal* division. They equitably distribute property acquired during the marriage or marital property. Non-marital property includes gifts or inheritances to one spouse during marriage or property acquired before marriage. However, non-marital property isn't necessarily safe from division. Equitable distribution states can divide pre- or post-marital assets.

Community property states divide community property equally. Separate property is property acquired by each spouse before marriage. Community property includes property acquired and used jointly or individually during the marriage. Separate property includes property one spouse owned before the marriage and retains sole title to after marriage, as well as property a spouse receives as a gift or inheritance before or during the marriage.

Separate property is not divided in divorce. If you exchange separate property for another asset, the new property continues as separate property, as does the sale proceeds. If you commingle separate property with joint property, the separate property becomes divisible joint property.

Spousal obligations incurred before marriage also remain separate obligations. The parties may agree to separately pay marital debts but this does not bind creditors who can nevertheless sue either spouse.

To protect property in a community property state, each spouse should list their separate property upon marriage. The spouses would formally agree that these assets are to remain separate property thereafter. Gifts or inheritances received during marriage should also be kept separate to keep these assets free from spousal claim.

How can I protect my assets from a spouse who may dissipate or conceal marital assets before the divorce?

Spouses who are most often cheated out of marital assets in divorce are usually those spouses who know too little about the family finances. Divorcing spouses can be dishonest. Asset searches by professional asset search firms don't always uncover concealed marital assets. A spouse can cleverly hide assets, particularly when the marriage had a long downturn and there is ample time to conceal assets. Spouses must stay alert to their spouse's business and financial affairs and also their ex-spouse's financial dealings after divorce. Ex-spouses may then discover earlier concealed assets. To hide assets, spouses sell stocks or bonds, or withdraw savings and claim the money was spent or lost. Or a spouse may title assets to a straw. Divorce courts routinely see these tactics and they can severely penalize the dishonest spouse.

Timing and fast-action are vital to protect assets when divorce looms. Spouses play 'hide and seek' with property. They transfer assets to international accounts, camouflage their ownership of assets, and sell business interest to friends or partners. Fraudulent asset transfers of business interests are notoriously common. The defrauded spouse can try to prove a fraudulent transfer, but the effort is usually futile or too expensive. And spouses may delay receiving income, inheritances or other assets until after they divorce. An accommodating employer, for instance, may defer a salary increase, bonus or large commission. Divorce promotes endless ways to hide assets and income.

How can a cohabitating couple avoid legal claims and property disputes?

This is a growing legal concern because many more couples now live together without marrying. Some want to test their relationship. Older folks may live together because marriage would disqualify them from social security or pensions. Others want to avoid responsibility for the care of an ill partner or the many other legal and financial complications that arise from marriage. These concerns become particularly acute when one party has substantially more wealth.

Cohabitating couples should have a cohabitation agreement to define the couple's rights to property. The agreement designates each party's separate property before cohabitation and provides for the distribution of assets acquired both jointly and singly during cohabitation. The cohabitation agreement may also resolve the responsibility for joint obligations, such as leases, utilities or insurance. Several palimony cases demonstrate that cohabitation agreements are as vital for cohabitating same sex couples as for heterosexual couples. Cohabitation agreements are also vital if one partner is considerably wealthier. This avoids the poorer partner's claim that the cohabitation was for personal care and services on the promise of compensation. A cohabitation agreement precisely defines the nature and purpose of the relationship and whether it involves compensation for services.

How can I lower huge legal fees when divorcing?

Divorce lawyers can consume one-third or more of a divorcing couple's assets. In a sense, you may need as much protection against huge legal fees as against spousal claims. Why fight to keep your assets from your spouse only to lose them to your lawyer? As with every legal battle, divorce can be unbelievably costly. So you must limit your costs before you do battle or you'll lose the war. First, hire an attorney well-experienced with divorces and who will also respect your desire for an economical, fast and relatively painless divorce. Secondly, shorten the battle and save a fortune in legal fees. Complete the divorce quickly! Don't let *your* lawyers needlessly prolong it with endless depositions and court appearances. These tactics only generate horrendous legal bills without a corresponding benefit. Thirdly, arbitrate or mediate. These are good, cost-effective alternatives to divorce court. Your spouse is probably as anxious as you to resolve the divorce and save legal fees. Fourthly, settle whatever points you can directly with your spouse. You can then more quickly reach agreement on unresolved issues. Finally, watch your lawyer's time. You can largely control legal costs. Don't make unnecessary demands on your lawyer's time.

Let's turn to the question of bankruptcy. What is its role in asset protection planning?

Bankruptcy is increasingly necessary for the financially-troubled individual and company. Over two million individuals and companies file bankruptcy annually; not a surprising statistic once you understand the role of bankruptcy to eliminate debts and protect assets. In a down economy, more debtors use bankruptcy to protect their wealth. We are a nation of debtors. Too many consumers are overburdened with credit card debts.

When should you consider bankruptcy?

Any debtor with *serious* financial problems should consider bankruptcy. However, bankruptcy isn't always the right answer. Bankruptcy is the answer only when you have too many debts to pay from your future income or from selling your assets. For example, why declare bankruptcy if you earn $100,000 a year and your debts are only $20,000? Short-term financial sacrifice on your part can pay down your excessive debts, and this is certainly preferable to bankruptcy. If your unsecured debts are less than 60 percent of your net annual pay, avoid bankruptcy. Commit 20 percent of your net pay to pay past creditors. Most creditors will wait two or more years if you show good faith and make systematic payments. Many more will settle for less. Consider bankruptcy only if you cannot completely eliminate your debts within three years.

Bankruptcy may also be necessary to protect your assets. In bankruptcy, all civil actions against you must immediately stop – whether they are lawsuits, IRS claims, seizures, levies, attachments, repossessions or foreclosures. Every creditor must observe the automatic stay of continued legal action imposed by bankruptcy. Bankruptcy provides you the opportunity to resolve your financial problems with creditors who would otherwise seize and sell your assets.

If I am sued wouldn't it make sense to simply file bankruptcy rather than defend against the claim?

Bankruptcy may be your best option if you are convinced you can't win and can't settle, or if you have few assets to lose in bankruptcy. The mere threat of bankruptcy may be enough to encourage litigants to settle favorably. But never file bankruptcy without first making every effort to resolve a case without bankruptcy. Bankruptcy should be your last resort, not your first.

What are the several types of bankruptcy?

There are several forms of bankruptcy; each is designed for individuals and businesses in different financial situations. Chapter 7 bankruptcy (straight or liquidating bankruptcy) erases all debts except those that are non-dischargeable. Conversely, you'll lose all your assets except those few assets that are exempt. You can file Chapter 7 as an individual or business. A corporation, partnership, trust or any other entity may file Chapter 7. Chapter 7 bankruptcy is the most popular bankruptcy and accounts for about 90 percent of all bankruptcies. When is Chapter 7 for you? If you have few non-exempt assets to lose, file Chapter 7. The big advantage of Chapter 7 is that your debts are forever extinguished. You start your life again debt-free.

Chapter 13, or the wage-earner plan, lets you keep your assets but does not discharge your debts. You instead repay your debts in part or in full over three to five years. Your repayment plan must pay creditors at least the amount they would receive under Chapter 7. Priority creditors, including taxing authorities, are usually fully paid. Secured creditors must receive an amount equal to the fair market value of their collateral. Chapter 13 is your remedy if you have non-exempt assets to save, such as a home with a large equity. If you have no assets or only exempt assets, then Chapter 13 probably isn't your remedy. Chapter 7 lets you keep your exempt assets and fully eliminate your debts.

Chapter 11 compares to Chapter 13 in that it also allows the debtor to keep his or her property while arranging a repayment plan with creditors. While a wage-earner plan is limited to employed individuals, Chapter 11 can be filed by any debtor. There is another important difference: Debtors in Chapter 13 cannot owe over $250,000 in unsecured debt and $750,000 in secured debt. There's no debt limit with Chapter 11. Farmers file Chapter 12, which is similar to Chapter 11.

You can also convert bankruptcies. For example, a company may be involuntarily petitioned into Chapter 7 and convert their case to Chapter 11. Or a company in Chapter 11 or wage-earner in Chapter 13 may convert to Chapter 7. This often happens when the debtor can't negotiate a satisfactory repayment plan or defaults on other bankruptcy obligations. It's important to select the right type of bankruptcy after consulting with an experienced bankruptcy attorney.

Are there timing factors to consider when filing bankruptcy?

Bankruptcy timing is critical. Debtors frequently file too soon or too late. In either instance, they lose possible benefits from their bankruptcy. Some tips: 1) Collect your tax refunds before you file. Tax refunds due to you when you file will be claimed by your trustee; 2) don't file bankruptcy too soon after paying a past debt if you want the creditor to keep the payment or the payments may be recoverable by the trustee as a voidable preference. Payments made within two years to relatives or other insiders are also recoverable; 3) if you anticipate future debts, then file after they can be discharged in bankruptcy. An example would be continuing medical costs due to an extended illness; 4) make certain you owned your home long enough to qualify for homestead protection before you file bankruptcy; 5) also wait to file if you incurred bills for non-essentials. More recent charges are not dischargeable.

What debts are not dischargeable in bankruptcy?

Bankruptcy won't extinguish every debt. Debts usually not dischargeable in bankruptcy include; 1) federal taxes less than three years old and state and local taxes; 2) child support and alimony; 3) student loans; 4) criminal fines and penalties (i.e. restitutions and traffic fines); 5) liabilities incurred through drunk driving; 6) withholding tax assessments; 7) dischargeable debts not listed on your bankruptcy schedules; and 8) debts incurred through fraud.

Debts not dischargeable in Chapter 7 bankruptcy may be dischargeable or resolved in Chapter 13. The bankruptcy court can also deny the discharge of other debts in Chapter 7 bankruptcy based upon the debtor's inequitable conduct. Secured debts and liens are dischargeable only to the extent the debt exceeds the value of the secured asset. Bankruptcy eliminates any remaining personal liability. The secured parties' rights become limited to the collateral's value and then their rights thereafter become the same as unsecured creditors.

What property is exempt in bankruptcy?

In Chapter 7 bankruptcy, the trustee liquidates the debtor's assets for the benefit of the debtor's creditors. However, an individual can keep certain property for the debtor to gain a fresh start. Whether property is exempt or non-exempt is important to both the debtor and the creditors. Exemptions were originally a matter of state law. Each state defined its exempt property. Congress then decided the states could use a federal list of exemptions. Some states required the debtor to use the state list of exemptions, others offered residents the option to choose the federal list of exemptions or the state's – depending upon which would be more advantageous to the resident. Before you file bankruptcy, you may convert non-exempt property into exempt property, or sell non-exempt property and use the proceeds to pay debts that wouldn't be dischargeable in bankruptcy, such as alimony or non-dischargeable taxes and student loans. These planning considerations are important. If you have significant assets, you must plan well ahead for bankruptcy.

Can bankruptcy stop foreclosure of my property or seizure of other assets by a judgment creditor?

Bankruptcy automatically stops creditor lawsuits, collections or repossessions. The automatic stay under bankruptcy further transfers pending or future collection and debtor-creditor cases from other courts to the bankruptcy court. Your creditors can't enforce prior judgments or liens against you or your property. However, criminal matters and suits to collect alimony or child support continue during bankruptcy.

The automatic stay also suspends a creditor's rights to repossess collateral. Still, a secured creditor can petition the bankruptcy court for permission to foreclose by requesting adequate protection. A secured creditor is any creditor with specific property as collateral to secure their debt. Mortgages on real estate, security interests on personal property or leases on equipment are examples. If a secured creditor requests adequate protection, the bankruptcy court must protect the creditor so his collateral isn't impaired or diminished by the automatic stay. This is important when collateral can lose value. The bankruptcy court then requires sufficient payment to the secured party to cover this depreciation. The creditor can repossess or foreclose on the collateral if there's no other way to protect the creditor. The automatic stay ends when the case is closed, dismissed or the debtor is discharged.

As you can see, bankruptcy won't always protect against foreclosure or repossession. You may file Chapter 11, for instance, to delay foreclosure and gain the opportunity to sell or refinance your property or to develop a reorganization plan to resolve the problem loan. But file bankruptcy with a realistic plan on how you will protect your secured creditor who holds liens against assets that you want to retain. You can abandon unwanted assets to your secured creditor. Any deficiency will become an unsecured debt dischargeable in your bankruptcy.

How can I protect my non-exempt assets in a bankruptcy?

The safest strategy is to convert unprotected assets into exempt assets. But you must then wait forty months before you file bankruptcy.

A well-drafted limited partnership or limited liability company should provide reasonable protection against a trustee's claim if you titled your assets to these entities at least two years prior to the bankruptcy. Similarly, a transfer to an irrevocable trust well prior to bankruptcy may succeed in sheltering your assets. Debtors also equity-strip exposed assets and use the mortgage proceeds to buy exempt assets, pay non-dischargeable debts, or pay preferred creditors.

Many protective strategies that can effectively shield assets from a judgment creditor will equally protect against a bankruptcy trustee. But it is dangerous to simply gift your property before bankruptcy. Gifts are easily recovered as fraudulent transfers. Transfers to family members or friends, even for a fair price, will be examined closely. Make certain any transfer is an honest, fair value transaction. Even an innocent transaction can be wrongly interpreted in bankruptcy and prevent your bankruptcy discharge. Review every major transaction within the preceding five years carefully with your attorney before you file. Finally, be scrupulously honest when you file bankruptcy. Don't attempt to conceal your ownership to assets. Bankruptcy fraud is a serious offense.

What other precautions do you recommend for debtors planning bankruptcy?

Involve an asset protection attorney in your planning. The interplay between asset protection and bankruptcy law can be extremely complex, and the new bankruptcy laws raise many unanswered questions. Often, bankruptcy attorneys think their role is simply to assist the client in having their papers completed properly, and on time, and to ensure that the entire process goes smoothly. In essence, they act as an intermediary between the client and the court and/or bankruptcy trustee. Many don't see it as their role to minimize the client's losses in bankruptcy. Some bankruptcy lawyers won't discuss defensive pre-bankruptcy planning strategies. They can 'throw you to the wolves' with little, if any, protection if they file too soon without adequately protecting you first.

What is your recommendation to avoid the potential loss of assets to the IRS?

We would give you these important pointers:

1) *Stay tax compliant.* Discipline yourself to get your tax filings done on time.
2) *Avoid tax shelters* or other aggressive schemes to sidestep taxes.
3) *File separate tax returns* if you are married. Why give both spouses exposure to the IRS?
4) *Cooperate* with the IRS. They too want to resolve your tax liability. But they are less likely to seize your assets if you responsibly address your tax situation.

5) *Protect your assets* before you have tax troubles. Of course, this warning prevails throughout this book!

12

YOUR NEXT AND MOST IMPORTANT STEP

Thank you for your insightful and educational interview. Now it's time to tell us more about your firm, The Presser Law Firm, P.A., and how it can help the reader achieve financial security.

The Presser Law Firm, P.A. is a national asset protection law firm. Asset protection and closely related services as estate planning and business and legal counsel is all we do. We design and implement strategies – both domestic and internationally – to effectively reposition and safeguard our clients' assets from litigation, creditor problems and other adverse claims. Typically, this is integrated into a comprehensive estate/financial plan.

Who are your typical clients?

Our clients come from all economic and occupational backgrounds. Typically, our clients have a net worth between $1-10 million; however, we represent a number of clients with more modest wealth, as well as many who are more affluent. A number of our clients are business firms that need protection against litigation.

Do you accept out-of-state clients?

Absolutely. The Presser Law Firm, P.A. is a nationwide firm. Our principal office is on the border of Boca Raton, Florida and Deerfield Beach, Florida; however, we represent clients from every state. Our out-of-state services are commonly handled via telephone and video conferencing. Where necessary, we work with local attorneys who are usually either the client's attorney or an in-state attorney selected by or affiliated with our own firm.

Do you also protect businesses?

Yes. About one-third of our clients require risk assessment and defensive planning for their family-owned business. We also have experienced business workout and debt-restructuring departments within our firm. It specializes in non-bankruptcy alternatives for the troubled company.

Do you accept referrals from other attorneys?

A good many of our clients are referred to us by other attorneys, accountants and financial professionals. And we work collaboratively with our clients' other professionals to assure that all our clients' legal and financial matters are well-coordinated.

Is it too late to use your services if I have already been sued or have financial troubles?

Not necessarily. Of course, as we say, you can best protect yourself when you plan before you have problems, but it's never too late to investigate your options when you need protection. Similarly, there are cases we do not accept. While most of our clients seek our services for legitimate purposes, we reject cases where we question the client's objectives or the prospective client's requests for services do not meet our standards.

What do you consider special about your firm?

First and most importantly, we specialize only in asset protection. That's all we do...and we do it well. We're extremely focused. Secondly, we're a boutique firm. When you call The Presser Law Firm, P.A., you have Attorney Mr. Presser to handle your case – not an associate. We truly care about our clients. We give them our personal attention. We know how emotionally unsettling it can be to have your wealth in jeopardy. The Presser Law Firm, P.A. clients know that with us on their side they have a true ally in resolving their problems.

How can our readers find out more about your firm, its services and how it can help them?

We enjoy hearing from our many readers. They can find more information about our firm at www.AssetProtectionAttorneys.com.

Our readers may also want to read our several other books on asset protection. Check www.BrooklinePress.com. Of course, we are delighted to have our readers attend one of our *Financial Self-Defense* seminars that we hold in various cities. We are also accepting offers to present at seminars, meetings and other events. Our presentation is strictly **educational**, and will outline many asset protection strategies that can be implemented the very same day. Please E-mail us at info@AssetProtectionAttorneys.com to request Asset Protection Attorneys to come to your business, seminar or other educational affair.

But, the best way to get started is to arrange a complimentary, preliminary, confidential consultation – either by phone or at our offices. We will review your situation and see how we can help you. It can be your most important step for a more secure financial future!

COMMIT TO YOUR FINANCIAL SECURITY TODAY...

TOMMOROW MAY BE TOO LATE!

Call Today 561-953-1050
or visit: www.AssetProtectionAttorneys.com

Put the ideas in this book to work for you. And to help you, I offer you a complimentary Financial Self-Defense preliminary consultation. This includes a personal conversation with me to evaluate your risk and financial exposure. To register for a complimentary preliminary consultation, please contact me via phone 561-953-1050, via website www.AssetProtectionAttorneys.com or via email info@AssetProtectionAttorneys.com. Call us today, tomorrow may be too late!

I would be pleased to discuss your situation, explain my services and how we can work together to achieve your goals. There's no cost or obligation for this preliminary, confidential consultation. I accept clients nationwide – both individuals and companies.

In addition to a complimentary preliminary consultation, I am offering a complimentary asset protection Monthly Newsletter subscription to those who email info@AssetProtectionAttorneys.com and mention the "Asset Protection Newsletter." The Monthly Newsletter contains **educational** information regarding asset protection such as Q and A's, changes in law, trending articles and more.

Finally, I will be holding in person and online workshops, seminars and webinars to educate the public on asset protection tactics and self-defense strategies. Please email The Presser Law Firm, P.A. and mention that you are "interested in learning more about our workshops and seminars" to be given dates and locations for upcoming workshops in your area or to book me for an **educational** seminar or speaking engagement at one of your upcoming events.

ABOUT THE AUTHOR

Hillel L. Presser, Esq., MBA represents individuals and businesses in connection with the establishment of comprehensive asset protection plans that incorporate both domestic and international components.

Hillel Presser has been featured in numerous newspapers and magazines, among them Forbes, Sports Illustrated, the Robb Report, the Houston Chronicle, and the Los Angeles Times. He has also appeared on several radio and television networks such as FOX, BRAVO, NBC, ABC, and CBS and has been profiled in the international press in Canada, Germany, Greece, Ireland, and the United Kingdom. He has represented some of today's most well-known business owners, celebrities and professional athletes.

Hillel Presser has authored several books and articles on Asset Protection and Law including Financial Self – Defense, The Lawyers Law of Attraction, Asset Protection Secrets, Financial Self – Defense (Revised Edition), Asset Protection in Financially Unsafe Times (foreword), and Captive Insurance Companies (foreword) just to name a few.

Hillel Presser graduated from the School of Management at Syracuse University where he was one of the first students to major in entrepreneurship. He then obtained his law degree from Nova Southeastern University where he was awarded the "Book Award" for the highest academic achievement in business entities and corporations. He has also completed his masters in marketing at Lynn University.

Hillel Presser sits on the President's Advisory Council and Ambassador Board for Nova Southeastern University and currently participates as an active board member for several non-profit organizations for some of his professional athlete clients. Mr. Presser also served as an Adjunct Faculty Member (Law) at Lynn University.

Hillel Presser grew up in Rochester, New York and now resides in Palm Beach County, Florida.

CONTACT THE AUTHOR

To obtain a **confidential** complimentary preliminary consultation regarding your assets.

To book Attorney Mr. Presser for a seminar, meeting or other speaking engagement.

To subscribe to The Presser Law Firm, P.A. online Financial Self-Defense Newsletter.

For any other questions regarding this book and asset protection.

Call Today 561-953-1050

or visit: www.AssetProtectionAttorneys.com

More Financial Self Defense Books from Brookline Press, LLC

- Financial Self Defense (Revised Edition)
- The Lawyers Law of Attraction
- So Sue Me!
- Asset Protection: The Professional Advisor's Guide
- How to Settle With the IRS for Pennies on the Dollar
- Offshore Wealth
- The Doctor's Wealth Protection Guide
- The Limited Partnership Book
- How to Protect Your Money Offshore
- Great Credit – Guaranteed
- Debt Free – Guaranteed
- Turnaround: Revitalizing the Troubled Company

... and other great titles available from Brookline Press, LLC (www.BrooklinePress.com)